Say Unto Wisdom

RESTORING BIBLICAL RELATIONSHIPS

Joseph Stephen

Faithful Generations

Copyright © 2015 by Joseph Stephen. All rights reserved.

No part of this book may be reproduced without written permission from the publisher or copyright holder, except in the case of brief quotations embodied in critical articles and reviews. No part of this book may be transmitted in any form or by any means—electronic, mechanical, photocopy, recording, or other—without prior written permission from the publisher or copyright holder.

All Scriptures are taken from The King James Version of the Holy Bible unless otherwise stated

ISBN-13: 978-0-9944042-1-3

Faithful Generations
South Australia, Australia
www.faithfulgeneration.com

Other books By Joseph Stephen include:

- The Sufficiency Of Scripture: The Key to Revival
- More Than Meets The Eye: Vision In Verse
- If A Picture Paints A Thousand Words: Give Your Child The Right Foundation For A Biblical Worldview
- The Perfect Programmer: A Christian Programming Curriculum
- Blindness, Braille And The Bible: A Christian Home Education Curriculum

Contents

Dedication	iv
Acknowledgements	iv
Foreword	v
Chapter 1. Introduction	1
Chapter 2. Behold The Fire And The Wood ...	5
Chapter 3. Am I My Brother's Keeper?	17
Chapter 4. The King Rose Up ...	23
Chapter 5. Say Unto Wisdom ...	29
Chapter 6. As Christ Loved The Church	33
Chapter 7. She Will Do Him Good ...	39
Chapter 8. Through Wisdom ...	42
Chapter 9. Mean What You Say	44
Chapter 10. The Tongue Is A Fire	52
Chapter 11. What Is Love?	56
Chapter 12. Who Is The Greatest?	63
Chapter 13. Family Worship And Discipleship	68
Chapter 14. What We Do In Private ...	84
Chapter 15. Dealing With Conflict	88
Chapter 16. How Many Times?	95
Chapter 17. Gratitude	100
Chapter 18. As It Hath Pleased Him	103
Chapter 19. Who Has Your Heart?	107
Chapter 20. Conclusion	117

Dedication

To my family – my dearest and cherished wife, and eight living children - God's most precious earthly gifts. In my sinful frailty, I have attempted to find out what I never knew, in order to teach you what I hope you'll never forget. My children, if the Lord so tarries, and grants you the blessings of marriage and children, may you teach your family these truths. May you enjoy in a deeper and richer way, the things we have only begun to learn.

Acknowledgements

Researching, writing, editing, formatting and proofreading a book is a huge task. I would like to thank the following people for their help in bringing this book to fruition:

- Dr Dallas Clarnette
- Dr Lance A. Box
- Mr Brent Grey
- Mr Michael Woolley
- Mr David D'Lima
- Mr Jean Engela
- Mr Theophilus Engela
- Mr Mervyn Harris
- my cherished wife Florence
- my eight precious children
- My Lord and Saviour, Jesus Christ

Foreword

Whilst I was working amongst the Warlpiri of Central Northern Territory, a senior elder spoke to me of the heartbreak that he and other elders felt because school teachers had taught the children of the community to address older people by their first name. The Warlpiri language, paralleling many other languages around the world, has a set of respect terms that need to be used when addressing others. These terms are terms of relationship, but also terms of deference. With the use of the respect language, there was an attitude and set of protocols that enabled appropriate interchange amongst the Warlpiri people. However, since the influence of Western schooling has been entrenched in the various Warlpiri communities, respect has broken down at all levels, and the old people lament.

This lamentation is felt by many of us who have been afflicted by the levelling forces of egalitarianism in Western culture. I have been a school teacher for 27 years, and I remember the days when students would address me as "Mr" or "Sir". I could get on and teach when respect had been established. In recent years, it became progressively more and more difficult to teach in a classroom (even classrooms of Christian schools) because there was no longer a culture of respect and deference.

There is an old adage that says, "You get what you preach." And again, it has been said, "The world follows the church." In many of the churches in the Western world, the fear of God has been lost, and with the loss of the fear of God, respectful relationships within the Church have also been lost. The world has taken its cue, and filled the vacuum with egalitarianism, feminism, children's rights, and so forth.

I commend Joseph Stephen in his efforts to reengage the church in a discussion of how we should live life with one another in a respectful way; a way that reflects a fear of God, a love for His Kingdom and His glory, and a trembling at His Word.

May God bless all those who seek to be doers of His Word, and who prayerfully apply the principles in this short book to the relationships that exist in the broader Christian community. And as we learn to love one another again, as Christ taught us to do, may the world come to know that Jesus is the Christ, the Son of the Living God.

- Dr Lance A. Box Jangala, PhD (Education)

Chapter 1

Introduction

In our current cultural environment, relationships have become incredibly shallow and impersonal. A room can be full of people texting others elsewhere, rather than relating in person to the people they are sitting next to. Our friendships are transient waves of likes and dislikes on Facebook. The depth of our words are a twitter tweet to inform everyone in cyberspace what we had for breakfast. We have fallen in love with technology to the point where Japan touts the first hotel staffed by robots[1], and the new Royal Adelaide hospital in South Australia will employ robots to perform many of the daily services such as the distribution of food and medicine[2]. Relationships have become fleeting, androgynous, egalitarian interactions via a touch screen. Gone is the personal touch of humanity, made in the image of a personal God (Gen. 1:26; Mat. 8:15; Mark 1:41; Luke 22:51; Heb. 4:15; 1 John 1:1. This is because though we all desire relationships, our sinful nature without God's guidance destroys

---

1 http://www.bbc.co.uk/newsround/33544583 accessed on 15 September 2015.
2 http://www.adelaidenow.com.au/news/robots-to-supply-drugs-food-at-new-rah/story-e6frea6u-1225969237042 accessed on 15 September 2015.

the very things we so deeply desire. How should we relate to each other?

I am no relationship expert. I came from a broken family. I never knew my biological father and yearn, like so many others, to know the love of my father. My mother married thrice and the incredible heartache of these and her other broken relationships have scarred me for life, not to mention deprived my children of a set of biological grandparents. I am not the perfect father myself, neither am I the perfect husband or son. Growing up, I never learned much about how to apply Biblical wisdom to any relationships until out of desperation, I sought the Lord as to how to be a father, when I had my own children.

Though I have commenced a journey of learning, this still does not make me an expert of any kind. What I share in this book is the wisdom of one who is an expert, the wisdom of the God who created relationships and who has given us the blueprint for their success. Knowing about such wisdom is of course half the battle. Knowing where we are going and what we are aiming for gives us the goals to work toward as we seek to raise our family or contribute to a local body of believers, which we shall see, is to glean its relational principles from the biological family. While reading the apostle Paul's letter to Timothy, the following verse caught my attention.

> Rebuke not an elder, but intreat him as a father; and the younger men as brethren; The elder women as mothers; the younger as sisters, with all purity. (1 Tim. 5:1-2.)

The apostle Paul previously taught that success as a father was a prerequisite qualification of an elder (1 Tim. 3:5). Now in chapter 5 he appeals to the foundation of family relationships to instruct the body of Christ in appropriate relationships within the assembly, the household of faith (Gal. 6:10).

In today's androgynous and egalitarian culture, these verses seem foreign to us. How should we entreat a father or mother? How should we treat a sister or brother? How does a father rule his own house well? What does it mean to have children in subjection? If all were identical in authority and role, the apostle Paul could have simply said, treat everyone with courtesy. Perhaps he could have restated the golden rule of Matthew 7:12, to do to others as we would have them do to us. Instead, the apostle draws our attention to our biological family in order to instruct us concerning our spiritual family. Thus we must have a Biblical understanding of God's design for the biological family in order to come to a correct understanding of relationships within the family of God.

Today, in Western nations at least, we have become accustomed to addressing all adults as equals regardless of age differences. In today's "modern, egalitarian" culture, adults think they do children a favour by allowing them to address them by their first name, supposing that they make themselves more approachable. In past generations, children would address adults using a respectful title which recognized the seniority of the adult. Once upon a time men would be discerning about what was appropriate to discuss in the presence of a lady. Their tone too would differ when talking to a lady compared to talking to another man. This was, no doubt, due to Biblical principles understood by former generations which have been forgotten. Today, men think they do women a service by sending them to the frontline of our physical and spiritual battles. Clearly the apostle Paul teaches us that there are distinctions to be made depending upon gender, age and role. These are not merely social or cultural conventions, but God ordained delineations designed to teach us to recognize and honour authority and to show appropriate respect.

If we look around at our churches today, we often see little difference between them and the world in terms of the prevalence of broken families, immorality, youth culture, the blurring of gender distinction, and individuality. Rediscovering the depth of God's design for relationships in our families and our local churches would transform our society tremendously. Christianity would have far more of an impact upon our culture if unbelievers could observe the consequences of living out God's rich wisdom in our daily interaction with one-another.

The first part of this book will investigate what relationships in the family and church should look like from a Biblical perspective. The second part will provide some practical Scriptural insights for nurturing such rich relationships.

Chapter 2

Behold The Fire And The Wood...

Before we look at how to entreat a father, we must investigate why we should entreat rather than demand of him as our equal. God ordained that the father be the head of the family unit. This is consistently true throughout the entire historic and prophetic timeline of the Scriptures.

- God created man first and then formed woman (Gen. 2:21-22).
- God formed woman in order to be a helper to Adam (Gen. 2:18).
- It is the man who leaves his father and mother to find a wife (Gen. 2:24) whereas the woman is given in marriage (see Gen. 34:9, 38:11; Lev. 22:13; Num. 30:3, 30:16; Deut. 22:21; Judg. 21:7; Ezra 9:12; Neh. 10:30; Ps. 78:63; Jer. 29:6; Luke 17:27, 20:34).
- God said that as part of the curse, man would rule over the woman (Gen. 3:16).
- God declares the law of headship of the father and husband (Num. 30).

- There are numerous references to heads of households and families being men.
- The Ten Commandments were addressed to men who in turn were to teach their families (Exod. 20) [thou shalt not covet thy neighbour's wife v.17 demonstrates that the commandments were addressed to men].
- The Lord Jesus chose twelve men as His apostles (Mt. 10:2).
- The apostle Paul reaffirms the creation order as relevant in the church age (1 Cor. 11:3, 1 Tim. 2:14).
- Elders and deacons are to be the husband of one wife (1 Tim. 3:2; Tit. 1:6; 1 Tim. 3:8-12).
- The 144,000 redeemed from the earth (Rev. 14:3-4) are men (having not been defiled with women).

Up until this past 150 years of history, this was accepted without question. This creation order is not about equality but about complementarity, and order of accountability and responsibility. The authority of the father as the head of his family is not given to wield unbridled power, but to protect, instruct, provide for and give direction to the family. This same honour was given to the father-in-law (see Exod. 18:7-24.)

God himself models the qualities of a good father for us to emulate. He is referred to as:

- a strong tower (Ps. 144:2);
- shelter (Ps. 61:3);
- refuge (Ps. 9:9, 14:6, 46:1);
- protecting wings (Ps. 17:8, 36:7, 57:1);
- rock, fortress, deliverer (Ps. 18:2);

- hiding place and shield (Gen. 15:1, Ps. 3:3, 28:7, 32:7, 91:4, 115:11, 119:114);
- shepherd (Ps. 23, John 10:11).

Though God is the perfect father, in the height of Israel's apostasy, God wrote the following by the pen of His prophet Malachi:

> A son honoureth his father, and a servant his master: if then I be a father, where is mine honour? and if I be a master, where is my fear? ... (Mal. 1:6a)

There was absolutely no question that a son should honour his father. God said, "A son honoureth his father." that was until the modern education system and mass media sowed the seed of disrespect, dishonour, egalitarianism and outright rebellion in the hearts and minds of this last couple of generations. Over the last century, Feminism has painted Christian men as misogynists, which unfortunately due to the abuse of authority and lack of recognition of what women did in the home, was not always unwarranted. However, the tide has turned, and the culture is now largely misandrist. Men are now painted as foolish, emasculated boneheads who need to be kept in line by their all-knowing tech-savvy children and high flying, career pursuing wife. Since Christians are also largely consumers of this mass-media propaganda, the church has largely followed the culture. Rather than the children entreating the father, the father must entreat his children.

Webster's English dictionary gives the meaning of entreat as: to ask (someone) in a serious and emotional way. To beg, ask, appeal to, petition, request, plead with, exhort, implore, enjoin, beseech, importune, ask earnestly, supplicate.

There are several notable accounts of children in the Scriptures that exemplify submission under the father's authority, given for our learning. I'd like to consider the accounts of Isaac, Jephthah's daughter, and the children of Rechab.

> And Abraham took the wood of the burnt offering, and laid it upon Isaac his son; and he took the fire in his hand, and a knife; and they went both of them together. And Isaac spake unto Abraham his father, and said, My father: and he said, Here am I, my son. And he said, Behold the fire and the wood: but where is the lamb for a burnt offering? And Abraham said, My son, God will provide himself a lamb for a burnt offering: so they went both of them together. And they came to the place which God had told him of; and Abraham built an altar there, and laid the wood in order, and bound Isaac his son, and laid him on the altar upon the wood. And Abraham stretched forth his hand, and took the knife to slay his son. (Gen 22:6-10.)

Isaac's unquestioning obedience is in stark opposition to the lack of respect and obedience shown to fathers today. Think for a moment how we would likely have answered our father back or at least put up quite a fight if we were in Isaac's position. What about how our son would react?

Isaac was not a little child. He was old enough to carry the wood for the sacrifice up a mountain at Moriah (Gen. 22:2; 22:6). He was no simpleton. He saw the fire and the wood and knew that they had not brought a lamb with them. He was certainly old enough to understand what was going on (Gen. 22:7.) I would even suggest that he may have been what we would consider an adult today. Even as his father bound him and laid him upon the altar, which he had no doubt helped to build; even as his father held the knife in his hand about to slay him, Isaac trusted his father and unwaveringly honoured him. This honour continued as he fully trusted his father's judgment in sending his most trusted servant to his father's kindred to find Isaac a wife (Gen. 24.) Today, we can just imagine what he might say, "No thanks dad, I'll pick my own wife, whether you approve of her or not. I don't like your choice of women!"

> And Jephthah vowed a vow unto the LORD, and said, If thou shalt without fail deliver the children of Ammon into mine hands, Then it shall be, that whatsoever cometh forth of the doors of my house to meet me, when I return in peace from the children of Ammon, shall surely be the LORD'S, and I will offer it up for a burnt offering. So Jephthah passed over unto the children of Ammon to fight against them; and the LORD delivered them into his hands. And he smote them from Aroer, even till thou come to Minnith, even twenty cities, and unto the plain of the vineyards, with a very great slaughter. Thus the children of Ammon were subdued before the children of Israel. And Jephthah came to Mizpeh unto his house, and, behold, his daughter came out to meet him with timbrels and with dances: and she was his only child; beside her he had neither son nor daughter. And it came to

pass, when he saw her, that he rent his clothes, and said, Alas, my daughter! thou hast brought me very low, and thou art one of them that trouble me: for I have opened my mouth unto the LORD, and I cannot go back. And she said unto him, My father, if thou hast opened thy mouth unto the LORD, do to me according to that which hath proceeded out of thy mouth; forasmuch as the LORD hath taken vengeance for thee of thine enemies, even of the children of Ammon. And she said unto her father, Let this thing be done for me: let me alone two months, that I may go up and down upon the mountains, and bewail my virginity, I and my fellows. And he said, Go. And he sent her away for two months: and she went with her companions, and bewailed her virginity upon the mountains. And it came to pass at the end of two months, that she returned unto her father, who did with her according to his vow which he had vowed: and she knew no man. And it was a custom in Israel, That the daughters of Israel went yearly to lament the daughter of Jephthah the Gileadite four days in a year. (Judg. 11:30-40.)

Jephthah's vow meant that his daughter would remain a virgin, unmarried, for the rest of her life. This was a cultural disgrace, unlike today, where even the church no longer encourages marriage in one's youth (Pr. 5:18; Mal. 2:14), let alone motherhood. We however do not read of his daughter rebelling, going off and leaving his jurisdiction and finding her own husband. We only read of a two month vacation which she took with the blessing of her father in order to mourn her loss of opportunity to get married.

And I set before the sons of the house of the Rechabites pots full of wine, and cups, and I said unto them, Drink ye wine. But they said, We will drink no wine: for Jonadab the son of Rechab our father commanded us, saying, Ye shall drink no wine, neither ye, nor your sons for ever: Neither shall ye build house, nor sow seed, nor plant vineyard, nor have any: but all your days ye shall dwell in tents; that ye may live many days in the land where ye be strangers. Thus have we obeyed the voice of Jonadab the son of Rechab our father in all that he hath charged us, to drink no wine all our days, we, our wives, our sons, nor our daughters; Nor to build houses for us to dwell in: neither have we vineyard, nor field, nor seed: But we have dwelt in tents, and have obeyed, and done according to all that Jonadab our father commanded us. … And Jeremiah said unto the house of the Rechabites, Thus saith the LORD of hosts, the God of Israel; Because ye have obeyed the commandment of Jonadab your father, and kept all his precepts, and done according unto all that he hath commanded you: Therefore thus saith the LORD of hosts, the God of Israel; Jonadab the son of Rechab shall not want (lack) a man to stand before me for ever. (Jer. 35:5-10, 18-19.)

The respect that Rechab's descendants showed their ancestor is incredible. This faithful respect did not last just one generation but continued for multiple generations. There was at least 200 years from the time of Rechab to this incident. (see 2 Sam. 4:2).

Consider too how Joseph commanded his family to carry his bones to the Promised Land before he died in Egypt in Gen. 50:25 and how Moses remembered this and took them with him from Egypt (see Ex. 13:19). His descendants eventually burying them after Joshua's death (see Josh. 24:32), more than two hundred years from the time of Joseph's death. Will our descendants care about, let alone remember what our wishes are two hundred years from now, if the Lord tarries?

All of these examples demonstrate that the respect of the father was taken extremely seriously. Indeed, this was the understanding of Ex. 20:12, to honour one's father and mother.

> Honour thy father and thy mother: that thy days may be long upon the land which the LORD thy God giveth thee. (Ex. 20:12.)

[The apostle Paul refers back to this commandment when reminding children to obey their parents and fathers to train their children in the nurture and admonition of the Lord (Eph. 6:1-4.)] This was so serious that God even legislated the death penalty for an adult child who continued to be a rebellious, gluttonous drunkard.

> If a man have a stubborn and rebellious son, which will not obey the voice of his father, or the voice of his mother, and that, when they have chastened him, will not hearken unto them: Then shall his father and his mother lay hold on him, and bring him out unto the elders of his city, and unto the gate of his place; And they shall say unto the elders of his city, This our son is stubborn and rebellious, he will not obey our voice; he is a glutton, and a

drunkard. And all the men of his city shall stone him with stones, that he die: so shalt thou put evil away from among you; and all Israel shall hear, and fear. (Deu. 21:18-21.)

Today we might think this harsh, and while we are not under this part of the Mosaic law, we'd do very well to recover the importance of respect for the patriarch of the family in our morally bankrupt, egalitarian culture.

It is fitting to take a moment to also consider the weight that the patriarch's word had upon subsequent generations. This is important because it was the glue of intergenerational continuity. Today words have little weight or meaning in terms of what a father may say by way of setting the course for the next generation. Perhaps the last vestige of such binding influence is the last will and testament. Even this however has been reduced to the doling out of material inheritance, not the casting of vision. Three such incidents are worth a mention.

> And it came to pass, as soon as Isaac had made an end of blessing Jacob, and Jacob was yet scarce gone out from the presence of Isaac his father, that Esau his brother came in from his hunting. And he also had made savoury meat, and brought it unto his father, and said unto his father, Let my father arise, and eat of his son's venison, that thy soul may bless me. And Isaac his father said unto him, Who art thou? And he said, I am thy son, thy firstborn Esau. And Isaac trembled very exceedingly, and said, Who? where is he that hath taken venison, and brought it me, and I have eaten of all before thou camest, and have blessed him? yea,

and he shall be blessed. And when Esau heard the words of his father, he cried with a great and exceeding bitter cry, and said unto his father, Bless me, even me also, O my father. And he said, Thy brother came with subtilty, and hath taken away thy blessing. And he said, Is not he rightly named Jacob? for he hath supplanted me these two times: he took away my birthright; and, behold, now he hath taken away my blessing. And he said, Hast thou not reserved a blessing for me? And Isaac answered and said unto Esau, Behold, I have made him thy lord, and all his brethren have I given to him for servants; and with corn and wine have I sustained him: and what shall I do now unto thee, my son? And Esau said unto his father, Hast thou but one blessing, my father? bless me, even me also, O my father. And Esau lifted up his voice, and wept. (Gen. 27:30-39.)

Ignoring for a moment that Jacob supplanted his brother, and that God called Esau profane for despising his birthright (Heb. 12:16), the fact was that Isaac could not retract or nullify his pronouncement. He had but one blessing, his word stood and was binding. The writer of Hebrews makes it clear that though Esau sought to reverse what had been done diligently with tears, Isaac's blessing was binding upon Jacob. The patriarch's blessing cast a vision or a curse upon the next generation and their declaration was respected as law.

In Gen. 49 we read of Jacob blessing his sons. His words are prophetic. While it seems that God revealed some of these predictions to Jacob, much of what he said were simply the observations of a father who knew the characters of his sons well. For example, Jacob's declaration that Reuben would not excel because he was unstable as water was because of Reuben's sin in defiling his father's bed (Gen. 22:35, 49:4).

Finally, when Jacob blesses Joseph's two sons, Jacob blesses the younger over the older:

> And Joseph brought them out from between his knees, and he bowed himself with his face to the earth. And Joseph took them both, Ephraim in his right hand toward Israel's left hand, and Manasseh in his left hand toward Israel's right hand, and brought them near unto him. And Israel stretched out his right hand, and laid it upon Ephraim's head, who was the younger, and his left hand upon Manasseh's head, guiding his hands wittingly; for Manasseh was the firstborn. And he blessed Joseph, and said, God, before whom my fathers Abraham and Isaac did walk, the God which fed me all my life long unto this day, The Angel which redeemed me from all evil, bless the lads; and let my name be named on them, and the name of my fathers Abraham and Isaac; and let them grow into a multitude in the midst of the earth. And when Joseph saw that his father laid his right hand upon the head of Ephraim, it displeased him: and he held up his father's hand, to remove it from Ephraim's head unto Manasseh's head. And Joseph said unto his father, Not so, my father: for this is the firstborn; put thy right hand upon his head. And his father refused, and said, I know it, my son, I know it: he also shall become a people, and he also shall be great: but truly his younger brother shall be greater than he, and his seed shall become a multitude of nations. (Gen. 48:12-19.)

Joseph did not tell his sons to disregard their senile grandfather's "mistake" but respected his elderly father's fully conscious choice to swap the blessing after initially questioning whether it was intentional. Nothing in the New Testament superseded the authority of the father nor the respect due him from his children. In terms of the Apostle Paul's original injunction to know how to entreat older men in the assembly, we must entreat them with the respect and honour with which we should entreat our own father.

CHAPTER 3

Am I My Brother's Keeper?

The Apostle Paul next instructs us to treat younger men as brothers. But how should we treat our biological brother? Until we understand this, we won't be able to understand what this really means.

> When thou sawest a thief, then thou consentedst with him, and hast been partaker with adulterers. Thou givest thy mouth to evil, and thy tongue frameth deceit. Thou sittest and speakest against thy brother; thou slanderest thine own mother's son. (Ps. 50:18-20.)

Did you notice which sin was equated with consenting to the actions of a thief and partaking with adulterers? Slandering one's brother, one's own mother's son. The slander or disrespect of one's brother is akin to condoning theft and adultery. This is a double-edged sword, not only do we do a disservice to our brother, but we also dishonour our mother: thou slanderest thine own mother's son. The Lord reinforced this in the gospels:

> Ye have heard that it was said of them of old time, Thou shalt not kill; and whosoever shall kill shall be in danger of the judgment: But I say unto you, That whosoever is angry with his brother without a cause shall be in danger of the judgment: and whosoever shall say to his brother, Raca (insults them), shall be in danger of the council: but whosoever shall say, Thou fool (curses them), shall be in danger of hell fire. (Mat. 5:21-22.)

The Lord Jesus was referring back to Leviticus 19:17. (Also see Lev. 25:25-41.)

> And the LORD said unto Cain, Where is Abel thy brother? And he said, I know not: Am I my brother's keeper? (Gen. 4:9.)

When Cain was questioned about the whereabouts of his brother Abel, he answered God with a sarcastic response, "Am I my brother's keeper?" God certainly expected him to be. This set the tone throughout Scripture.

Indeed, Abraham treated his nephew better than many treat their own brother today. When their cattle and possessions grew too numerous to remain together, they separated, Abraham offering his nephew first pick of the best land (Gen. 13:8-11.) Then, when Lot was captured in battle, Abraham armed his servants and pursued Lot's captors (Gen. 14:14-16.) The Psalmist also praises the pleasantness of brethren dwelling together in unity.

Behold, how good and how pleasant it is for brethren to dwell together in unity! It is like the precious ointment upon the head, that ran down upon the beard, even Aaron's beard: that went down to the skirts of his garments; As the dew of Hermon, and as the dew that descended upon the mountains of Zion: for there the LORD commanded the blessing, even life for evermore. (Ps. 133:1-3.)

The fresh, life-giving dew of Mount Hermon revitalized everything growing on the mountain. Would we describe what emanates from our brotherly interaction in the home or church as pleasant, refreshing, fragrant ointment?

Some of the positive relationships between siblings mentioned in Scripture include:

- Moses and Aaron (Exod. 4:14),
- Joseph and Benjamin (Gen. 43:34),
- James and John (are mentioned together on many occasions),
- Simon and Andrew (Mark 1:29),
- Matthew and James (both sons of Alphaeus, Mat. 10:3; Mark 2:14).

The verse below reminds us that even though a friend loves through thick and thin, brothers particularly are born for times of adversity.

A friend loveth at all times, and a brother is born for adversity. (Prov. 17:17.)

We are warned of the difficulty of trying to win back a brother whom we have offended:

> A brother offended is harder to be won than a strong city: and their contentions are like the bars of a castle. (Prov. 18:19.)

Perhaps that is why the Apostle Paul pleaded with the Ephesians as he did.

> With all lowliness and meekness, with longsuffering, forbearing one another in love; Endeavouring to keep the unity of the Spirit in the bond of peace. (Eph. 4:2-3.)

James also writes much about dealing with strife amongst brethren in the assembly.

> Who is a wise man and endued with knowledge among you? Let him shew out of a good conversation his works with meekness of wisdom. But if ye have bitter envying and strife in your hearts, glory not, and lie not against the truth. This wisdom descendeth not from above, but is earthly, sensual, devilish. For where envying and strife is, there is confusion and every evil work. But the wisdom that is from above is first pure, then peaceable, gentle, and easy to be intreated, full of mercy and good fruits, without partiality, and without hypocrisy. And the fruit of righteousness is sown in peace of them that make peace. (James 3:13-18.)

Some of the brotherly relationships which fell into the above category include:

- Cain and Abel: (Gen. 4:3-10)
- Ishmael and Isaac: (Gen. 21:8-9)
- Jacob and Esau: (Gen. 25:22-26, 27:41-42)
- Joseph and his brothers: (Gen. 37, 45:1-15)
- David and his brothers: (1 Sam. 17:17-29)
- Barnabas and Paul: (Acts 15:39-40)

Men particularly are prone to contention due to them having that God ordained leadership in their genetic programming. Solomon puts it like this.

> Iron sharpeneth iron; so a man sharpeneth the countenance of his friend. (Prov. 27:17.)

When iron sharpens iron, sparks fly! This is why we must be careful to understand how to moderate our conduct in the church with respect to age and gender by first understanding how such familial relationships should be. The apostle John also wrote of the importance of good brotherly relations, both biological and spiritual:

> He that saith he is in the light, and hateth his brother, is in darkness even until now. He that loveth his brother abideth in the light, and there is none occasion of stumbling in him. But he that hateth his brother is in darkness, and walketh in darkness, and knoweth not whither he goeth, because that darkness hath blinded his eyes. (1 John 2:9-11.)

> We know that we have passed from death unto life, because we love the brethren. He that loveth not his brother abideth in death. Whosoever hateth his brother is a murderer: and ye know that no murderer hath eternal life abiding in him. (1 John 3:14-15.)

> If a man say, I love God, and hateth his brother, he is a liar: for he that loveth not his brother whom he hath seen, how can he love God whom he hath not seen? (1 John 4:20.)

Clearly God places incredible importance on the relationship between siblings, in the family in particular, and thus also within the church, the household of faith (Gal. 6:10.)

CHAPTER 4

The King Rose Up...

The Apostle then tells us to treat older women as mothers. The mother is to be highly honoured. The phrase "his mother's name was ..." occurs at least 30 times throughout the Scriptures in conjunction with the mention of the name of kings. This reflected the importance of the mother's influence on the raising of the king. Solomon, the wisest and richest king that ever lived, bowed in respect to his mother, even in his office as the king, the highest human authority in the nation.

> Bathsheba therefore went unto king Solomon, to speak unto him for Adonijah. And the king rose up to meet her, and bowed himself unto her, and sat down on his throne, and caused a seat to be set for the king's mother; and she sat on his right hand. (1 Kings 2:19.)

This honour of father and mother is of course codified in the Ten Commandments as already mentioned. We are to obey the law of our mother (so long as that law does not violate God's law). (Prov. 1:8, 6:20.) Interestingly, we read of two children who obeyed their mother even though what they asked their child to do was in violation of God's law, but such was their respect for their mother. The first example is that of Jacob and Rebekah. Though Jacob questions his mother's intention of deceit, yet he obeys.

> My father peradventure will feel me, and I shall seem to him as a deceiver; and I shall bring a curse upon me, and not a blessing. And his mother said unto him, Upon me be thy curse, my son: only obey my voice, and go fetch me them. (Gen. 27:12-13.)

The second instance which comes to mind is that of Herodias's daughter. In that instance, the daughter didn't even question her mother's evil request, such was her respect.

> But when Herod's birthday was kept, the daughter of Herodias danced before them, and pleased Herod. Whereupon he promised with an oath to give her whatsoever she would ask. And she, being before instructed of her mother, said, Give me here John Baptist's head in a charger. (Mat. 14:6-8.)

Just as Isaac respected his father's choice of a wife, we read that Ishmael's mother helped him find a wife in the absence of his father (Gen. 21:21.) We live in a society which seems to despise mothers-in-law. Mothers-in-law, however, were treated like one's own mother. Both Orpah and Ruth demonstrated their love for their mother-in-law

(Ruth 1:14.) While Naomi convinced Orpah to return to her people, Ruth could not be convinced to leave and remained with her mother-in-law. Her words are worth quoting here to show her beautiful loyalty:

> And Ruth said, Intreat me not to leave thee, or to return from following after thee: for whither thou goest, I will go; and where thou lodgest, I will lodge: thy people shall be my people, and thy God my God: Where thou diest, will I die, and there will I be buried: the LORD do so to me, and more also, if ought but death part thee and me. (Ruth 1:16-17.)

In the book of Proverbs, Solomon reveals the wisdom of God in his many references to the importance of children honouring their mother:

> A wise son maketh a glad father: but a foolish man despiseth his mother. (Prov. 15:20.)

> He that wasteth his father, and chaseth away his mother, is a son that causeth shame, and bringeth reproach. (Prov. 19:26.)

> Whoso curseth his father or his mother, his lamp shall be put out in obscure darkness. (Prov. 20:20.)

The above verse appears to be a reference to Deut. 21:18-21 which we mentioned earlier. The word obscure is very strong. It means deep darkness, pitch blackness, it refers to the utter shame of someone whose life is expunged and whose memory is obliterated because of their utterly deprave behaviour. That utterly despicable behaviour was not murder, but cursing one's parents.

> Hearken unto thy father that begat thee, and despise not thy mother when she is old. (Prov. 23:22.)

The above verse has a double emphasis in it, "thy father," and "who begat thee." Of course a father begets someone but the double emphasis is there to impress the fact that it was your father and mother who brought you into the world, so harken to them and especially do not despise your mother when she is old.

> Whoso robbeth his father or his mother, and saith, It is no transgression; the same is the companion of a destroyer. (Prov. 28:24.)

Why is such an one a destroyer? One who shows such contempt for one's father or mother will not carry their teaching or values forward to the next generation. They are in effect destroying the next generation because of their disrespect for the prior generation. If their parents were teaching them the law of God, then the next generation would not be taught God's ways and therein lies the destruction.

> There is a generation that curseth their father, and doth not bless their mother. (Prov. 30:11.)

"There is a generation that does not bless their mother." This suggests that normal behaviour is to continually be blessing one's mother. According to Webster's dictionary, the word bless means to exalt, invoke happiness on, praise, thank, magnify, extol, to provide someone with something good or desirable.

> The eye that mocketh at his father, and despiseth to obey his mother, the ravens of the valley shall pick it out, and the young eagles shall eat it. (Prov. 30:17.)

The above proverb is very profound. It means that one who mocks his father or despises to obey his mother will literally never see what is good for them because they'll be blinded to the truth. They'll be robbed and taken advantage of by those with evil motive. They'll reap the destructive consequences of despising God's wisdom, and God's dispensers of that wisdom, parents. When we consider all of these verses in light of our starting verse, we realize the great respect with which we ought to treat older women in the church. Even the Lord himself gave us an incredible example of requiting his earthly mother when from the depths of His anguish and agony, from His very cross, He committed the care of His mother into the care of the disciple whom He loved most.

> Now there stood by the cross of Jesus his mother, and his mother's sister, Mary the wife of Cleophas, and Mary Magdalene. When Jesus therefore saw his mother, and the disciple standing by, whom he loved, he saith unto his mother, Woman, behold thy son! Then saith he to the disciple, Behold thy mother! And from that hour that disciple took her unto his own home. (John 19:25-27.)

It is important to realize that the Lord Jesus had at least six earthly siblings (see Matthew 13:55-56 where sisters are mentioned in the plural, i.e. at least two, and four brothers are named), yet he entrusted the care of his earthly mother to His favourite disciple, John, not to His earthly brothers. This may have been because his brethren did not believe in Him yet (John 7:5.)

Chapter 5

Say Unto Wisdom...

Finally, the apostle Paul tells us to treat younger women as sisters with all purity. Let us consider the depth of this directive.

> Say unto wisdom, Thou art my sister; and call understanding thy kinswoman: That they may keep thee from the strange woman, from the stranger which flattereth with her words. (Prov. 7:4-5.)

The immediate context of this verse teaches us that a sister looks out for the purity of her brother, just as a brother is to help protect the purity of his sister. We see examples of the reverse of Proverbs 7:5 in the accounts of Dinah and Tamar. In Gen. 34:7-31, Dinah's brothers take revenge on Shechem and his people because he defiled Dinah. In 2 Samuel 13, Tamar is defiled by Amnon her half-brother, and is then cared for by her brother Absalom who eventually takes revenge on Amnon. (2 Sam. 13:20, 13:28-29.) While the revenge in both cases took things too far, vengeance being God's (Rom. 12:19), yet in both cases, the protective actions of the brothers is highly commendable. We also see the role of a brother as a sister's guardian illustrated in Song of Solomon:

> We have a little sister, and she hath no breasts: what shall we do for our sister in the day when she shall be spoken for? If she be a wall, we will build upon her a palace of silver: and if she be a door, we will inclose her with boards of cedar. (Sol. 8:8-9.)

The New Living Translation's paraphrase sheds light on this seemingly obscure verse:

> We have a little sister too young for breasts. What will we do if someone asks to marry her? If she is chaste, we will strengthen and encourage her. But if she is promiscuous, we will shut her off from men. (Sol. 8:8-9 NLT.)

Beyond the immediate context of Proverbs 7:4-5, however is something quite profound. Why did God, through Solomon's pen, tell us to "Say unto wisdom, thou art my sister?" We begin to get a glimpse of the meaning of this verse when we consider the preciousness of wisdom.

> Wisdom is the principal thing; therefore get wisdom: and with all thy getting get understanding. Exalt her, and she shall promote thee: she shall bring thee to honour, when thou dost embrace her. She shall give to thine head an ornament of grace: a crown of glory shall she deliver to thee. (Prov. 4:7-9.)

How much better is it to get wisdom than gold! and to get understanding rather to be chosen than silver! (Prov. 16:16.)

For wisdom is better than rubies; and all the things that may be desired are not to be compared to it. (Prov. 8:11.)

What we learn is that wisdom is to be treasured above all, and protected at any cost. We learn of its immense value. We are taught that if embraced, wisdom brings one to honour, that it is an ornament of grace and a crown of glory. Then we are taught that wisdom is to be regarded as one's sister. Could you imagine this to mean that you should treat wisdom as that sister you despise and always compete and fight with? I think not. Just as one highly treasures, cherishes and protects one's sister, one should treasure and highly prize wisdom. The paraphrase of the New Living Translation says it well, "Love wisdom like a sister." Do we regard wisdom as a treasure to be sought after and guarded? Do we treat our sister with the same preciousness as wisdom?

We also see how wisdom becomes a garland of glory to those who embrace her, similar to how a sister should bring out the best in her brother. She should seek his best rather than compete with him, becoming his crown of glory rather than his rival.

The Song of Solomon refers to both sister and spouse in the same sentence (Sol. 4:9-10, 4:12, 5:1-2.) This is not condoning marrying one's sister, which was legal until the giving of the law (see Gen. 12:13, 20:12, cp. Lev. 18:9), rather, this reveals that husband and wife can be far more than just physically close. It demonstrates that husband and wife can enjoy the same depth of loyalty and understanding that a brother and sister should enjoy. Unfortunately, in this sexually charged culture in which we live, our concept of relationship has been perverted so that when we talk of intimacy, all we think of is physical. That is partly why our divorce rate is so high. Bringing this back to our original verse, just as we should treasure, cherish and protect our biological sister with all purity, so too we should cherish and treat younger women in the church, with all purity.

Chapter 6

As Christ Loved The Church

Bible critics have cited examples of polygamy and brutality of wives to bolster their hatred of God who they claim is a first class misogynist. The examples often cited refer to the sinful actions of men and not the will or commandment of God. Indeed if the Bible were a fairy tale, it certainly wouldn't include all of the failings of man. Out of all of the relationships described in the Bible, the most challenging one must surely be the analogy of Christ's love for His church, as the picture of how the husband ought to love his wife.

> Husbands, love your wives, even as Christ also loved the church, and gave himself for it; That he might sanctify and cleanse it with the washing of water by the word, That he might present it to himself a glorious church, not having spot, or wrinkle, or any such thing; but that it should be holy and without blemish. So ought men to love their wives as their own bodies. He that loveth his wife loveth himself. For no man ever yet hated his own flesh; but nourisheth and cherisheth it, even as the Lord the church: For we are members of his body, of his flesh, and of his bones. For this cause

shall a man leave his father and mother, and shall be joined unto his wife, and they two shall be one flesh. (Eph. 5:25-31.)

Christ gave us an incredible example. It is a far cry from the couch potato, slothfully lazing on the sofa watching footy, shouting out for his sheila to bring him his six-pack of beer, which is often how the media portrays the average Australian male.

Now before the feast of the passover, when Jesus knew that his hour was come that he should depart out of this world unto the Father, having loved his own which were in the world, he loved them unto the end. And supper being ended, the devil having now put into the heart of Judas Iscariot, Simon's son, to betray him; Jesus knowing that the Father had given all things into his hands, and that he was come from God, and went to God; He riseth from supper, and laid aside his garments; and took a towel, and girded himself. After that he poureth water into a bason, and began to wash the disciples' feet, and to wipe them with the towel wherewith he was girded. ... So after he had washed their feet, and had taken his garments, and was set down again, he said unto them, Know ye what I have done to you? Ye call me Master and Lord: and ye say well; for so I am. If I then, your Lord and Master, have washed your feet; ye also ought to wash one another's feet. For I have given you an example, that ye should do as I have done to you. Verily, verily, I say unto you, The servant is not greater than his lord; neither he that is sent greater than he that sent him. If ye know these things, happy are ye if ye do them. (John 13:1-5, 12-17)

Of course this pales into insignificance when compared to the laying down of his life.

> Greater love hath no man than this, that a man lay down his life for his friends. (John 15:13.)

> For scarcely for a righteous man will one die: yet peradventure for a good man some would even dare to die. But God commendeth his love toward us, in that, while we were yet sinners, Christ died for us. (Rom. 5:7-8.)

This is a high calling and one I am constantly challenged by. It is easy to lust after one's wife but much harder to love her sacrificially, especially when the flower of one's youth begins to wane.

> Likewise, ye husbands, dwell with them according to knowledge, giving honour unto the wife, as unto the weaker vessel, and as being heirs together of the grace of life; that your prayers be not hindered. (1 Peter 3:7.)

Regardless of what feminism says, God tells us husbands to honour our wife as the weaker vessel. We often think of this solely in terms of physique. We forget however that we are wired differently emotionally. As husbands we need to stop the propagation of the feminist competition agenda and rather cherish and protect the helper whom God deliberately designed to be our complement, not our opponent. Indeed women can be physically strong, Sarah must have been, in order to follow Abraham in his journey. They are also emotionally strong, especially those who have borne many children, yet they are described as the "weaker vessel." This perhaps could also refer to her inability to resist subtle deception as alluded to in 1 Tim. 2:14.

> Husbands, love your wives, and be not bitter against them. (Col. 3:19.)

Have you ever considered the love Adam had for his wife? His wife was deceived into sinning, but Adam knowingly sinned. Why? He knew the command and penalty pronounced by God, death. All we can conclude from this account when carefully considering Adam's actions is that because he loved his wife so much, he gave up his life to endure the same penalty as she. The only alternative for him was separation from his beloved. While the Bible does not spell this out, we must understand that he was not Homer Simpson, a muddle-headed dunce, he was the most intelligent man who ever lived; and he knew full well the consequences of disobedience, yet he chose to take the fruit with his wife. After judgment was pronounced, he did blame his wife (as all men did after his example), yet he clearly chose to eat of the fruit of the knowledge of good and evil as a conscious decision. Of course It could be argued that he should have taken the lead and helped his wife avoid the serpent's temptation but remember, up until Gen. 3:16, while the woman was created as his help meet, until she was deceived, Adam was not her master. The headship of man over his wife as a protective covering, was only pronounced as a result of the fall, perhaps as an act of mercy to protect her from further deception.

We have already seen from our discussion of sisters and mothers that women are to be protected, not sent to the frontlines of our physical or spiritual battles. Some examples from Scripture include:

- The children of Gad and Reuben fought but left their children and wives in the protection of fenced cities (Numbers 32:6, 32:17-26);
- David rescued his wife, Abigail who had been taken captive (1 Samuel 30:5-18);
- Mordecai took care of his uncle's daughter Esther after her parents' death (Est. 2:5-7);
- Nehemiah commanded the men to fight for their children, wives, and property (Nehemiah 4:14);

In the one case where a woman went to battle, she recognized that it was dishonouring that a woman should do what should have been done by a man:

> And she said, I will surely go with thee: notwithstanding the journey that thou takest shall not be for thine honour; for the LORD shall sell Sisera into the hand of a woman. And Deborah arose, and went with Barak to Kedesh. (Judges 4:9.)

This also applies to spiritual battles. Elders are to be the husband of one wife (i.e. male), as are teachers (women are to remain silent in the church, and not usurp the authority of the man). They can of course be prayer warriors, but we should not expect nor send our women to the frontline. The apostle reiterates why this is the case:

> But I suffer not a woman to teach, nor to usurp authority over the man, but to be in silence. For Adam was first formed, then Eve. And Adam was not deceived, but the woman being deceived was in the transgression. (1 Timothy 2:12-14.)

Since these verses apply to sisters, they have a direct bearing upon how we treat women in the church in terms of our expectations of what they should be doing. Their primary role is as helpers to their own husbands, being mothers, showing hospitality, teaching younger women how to love their husband and children, helping with other people's children, helping with the elderly, etc. All of the verses cited in the prior three sections on how to treat mothers, sisters and wives demonstrate that God's view of women and the respect owed to them is much higher than that claimed by Bible critics.

CHAPTER 7

She Will Do Him Good

While much has been written on the subject of godly submission, we include this section for completeness. If we as husbands would love our wives as Christ loved the church, selflessly, completely and purely, submission would be more of a joy than a burden for our wives. But neither the command to the husband to love his wife, nor the command to the wife to come under the husband's protective headship are conditional or optional, and both are written with full knowledge of our frail, sinful humanity in view.

> That they may teach the young women to be sober, to love their husbands, to love their children, To be discreet, chaste, keepers at home, good, obedient to their own husbands, that the word of God be not blasphemed. (Titus 2:4-5.)

One thing many aren't taught when preparing for marriage is that loving one's husband does not come easy. Many men are hard to love. Once the emotion and chemistry is overwhelmed by the responsibilities of children and the daily grind, the reality of living with another selfish sinful person sets in. Even as Christians who desire to submit to the Lordship of Christ, we never completely shake off our sinful nature this side of heaven. Yet, marriage is for life.

> Wives, submit yourselves unto your own husbands, as unto the Lord. For the husband is the head of the wife, even as Christ is the head of the church: and he is the saviour of the body. (Eph. 5:22-23.)

> Likewise, ye wives, be in subjection to your own husbands; that, if any obey not the word, they also may without the word be won by the conversation of the wives; While they behold your chaste conversation coupled with fear. Whose adorning let it not be that outward adorning of plaiting the hair, and of wearing of gold, or of putting on of apparel; But let it be the hidden man of the heart, in that which is not corruptible, even the ornament of a meek and quiet spirit, which is in the sight of God of great price. For after this manner in the old time the holy women also, who trusted in God, adorned themselves, being in subjection unto their own husbands: Even as Sara obeyed Abraham, calling him lord: whose daughters ye are, as long as ye do well, and are not afraid with any amazement. (1 Peter 3:1-6.)

> The heart of her husband doth safely trust in her, so that he shall have no need of spoil. She will do him good and not evil all the days of her life. (Prov. 31:11-12.)

> Let the husband render unto the wife due benevolence: and likewise also the wife unto the husband.

The wife hath not power of her own body, but the husband: and likewise also the husband hath not power of his own body, but the wife. Defraud ye not one the other, except it be with consent for a time, that ye may give yourselves to fasting and prayer; and come together again, that Satan tempt you not for your incontinency. (1 Cor. 7:3-5.)

And the woman which hath an husband that believeth not, and if he be pleased to dwell with her, let her not leave him. For the unbelieving husband is sanctified by the wife, and the unbelieving wife is sanctified by the husband: else were your children unclean; but now are they holy. But if the unbelieving depart, let him depart. A brother or a sister is not under bondage in such cases: but God hath called us to peace. (1 Cor. 7:13-15.)

The Scriptures describe such a situation where the wife was a godly woman but her husband evil. Abigail's account is given in 1 Samuel 25:2-38. We are not told how long Abigail was married to this evil man. Her conduct however, was not conditional on his treatment of her. God, in His time, dealt with that man and relieved her of his evil. One cannot help the situation where one is saved after marriage and their spouse remains unsaved, but as Christians, we should never even entertain the thought of marrying an unbeliever. We must also help our children choose a spouse who bears the fruit of their professed faith, not just marry one who claims to be a Christian and perhaps goes to church on Sunday, yet has no interest in the things of the Lord outside of that time. This of course presupposes that our children also bear the fruit of genuine faith.

CHAPTER 8

Through Wisdom

> Through wisdom is an house builded; and by understanding it is established: And by knowledge shall the chambers be filled with all precious and pleasant riches. (Prov. 24:3-4.)

Relationships of the depth described in this book do not happen by accident. Any relationship can only reach its full potential when all parties willingly submit to the Lordship of Christ, the author of all relationships, and then submit to one-another according to God's creation order.

When this verse speaks of the chambers being filled with all precious and pleasant riches, it is easy to immediately think of material riches because of our materialistic and affluent culture. However, if we consider this just a bit deeper, we'll realize that there are no riches more precious nor pleasant than godly family relationships. It is by knowledge, wisdom and selfless submission that our rooms will be filled with such treasures. When our homes start exuding such pleasantness, our church relationships will be blessed beyond measure as a result.

The following chapters outline some of the practical principles which will help in developing the Biblical relationships discussed thus far. What I hope becomes clear, is that we must deliberately and diligently nurture a culture of discipleship in our homes and in our local church, so that the wisdom of the older is communicated to the younger. Rather than age segregated activities, we should encourage the interaction of whole families whenever practical.

Chapter 9

Mean What You Say

Be a Man of Your Word
(From More than Meets The Eye, Copyright 2015 by Joseph Stephen)

Be a man of your word!
Mean what you say.
Think twice before speaking,
Before committing your way.
Be a man of your word!
It's too common today,
to go back on our promise,
to forget what we say.

When Isaac blessed Jacob,
Though Jacob deceived him,
His blessing was binding,
It could not be retracted.
Though Esau repented,
The blessing was given,
Though Esau wept bitter,
It was bound in heaven.

Then Jephthah the warrior
Vowed that he'd offer
The first one to meet him,
If God helped him win.
His dear only daughter
Came dancing with timbrels.
He still kept his promise,
Though it crushed him within.

Words flow like water,
It happens too often,
We promise our help,
We promise to pray.
We'd do well to remember,
Each idle word uttered,
We must give an account of
At the great judgment day.

Trust is the most fundamental principle of any relationship. Indeed, we take its importance for granted. The basic meaning of trust is simply that we can rely upon one's word. Marriage is based upon trust. Once trust is broken, relationships crumble.

While words have almost become meaningless in the culture around us due to the influence of post-modern deconstructionism, Christians, of all people, should exemplify the Biblical truth that words have meaning. In particular, our words should be binding. If we promise our wife to be loyal in sickness and health, those words do not become void the minute we find someone more able to fulfil our carnal desires. When we give our children the "last warning," they know that often we don't really mean what we say. As time goes on, they know just how far they can push us before we snap in anger. The reason why our churches are full of individuals whose words of commitment, help and sympathy often fail when it really counts, is because within the family, our words also no longer have meaning. If our relationships in the church are to improve, we must begin to be as serious about our words in the family as the Bible demonstrates they should be. The following accounts will help demonstrate just how much weight a man's words had.

> And when the inhabitants of Gibeon heard what Joshua had done unto Jericho and to Ai, They did work wilily, and went and made as if they had been ambassadors, and took old sacks upon their asses, and wine bottles, old, and rent, and bound up; And old shoes and clouted upon their feet, and old garments upon them; and all the bread of their provision was dry and mouldy. And they went to Joshua unto the camp at Gilgal, and said unto him, and to the men of Israel, We be come from a far country: now therefore make ye a league with us. And the men of Israel said unto the Hivites, Peradventure ye dwell among us; and how shall we make a league with you? And they said unto Joshua, We are thy servants. And Joshua said unto them, Who are ye? and from whence come ye? And they said unto him, From a very far country thy servants are come because of the name of the LORD thy God: for we have heard the fame of him, and all that he did in Egypt, And all that he did to the two kings of the Amorites, that were beyond Jordan, to Si-

hon king of Heshbon, and to Og king of Bashan, which was at Ashtaroth. ... And the men took of their victuals, and asked not counsel at the mouth of the LORD. And Joshua made peace with them, and made a league with them, to let them live: and the princes of the congregation sware unto them. And it came to pass at the end of three days after they had made a league with them, that they heard that they were their neighbours, and that they dwelt among them. And the children of Israel journeyed, and came unto their cities on the third day. Now their cities were Gibeon, and Chephirah, and Beeroth, and Kirjathjearim. And the children of Israel smote them not, because the princes of the congregation had sworn unto them by the LORD God of Israel. And all the congregation murmured against the princes. But all the princes said unto all the congregation, We have sworn unto them by the LORD God of Israel: now therefore we may not touch them. This we will do to them; we will even let them live, lest wrath be upon us, because of the oath which we sware unto them. And the princes said unto them, Let them live; but let them be hewers of wood and drawers of water unto all the congregation; as the princes had promised them. (Josh. 9:3-10, 14-21.)

Many years later, in the time of King David, this league became a thorn in Israel's side.

Then there was a famine in the days of David three years, year after year; and David enquired of the LORD. And the LORD answered, It is for Saul, and for his bloody house, because he slew the Gibeonites. And the king called the Gibeonites, and said unto them; (now the Gibeonites were not of the children of Israel, but of the remnant of the Amorites; and the children of Israel had sworn unto them: and Saul sought to slay them in his zeal to the children of Israel and Judah.) Wherefore David said unto the Gibeonites, What shall I do for you? and wherewith shall I make the atonement, that ye may bless the inheritance of the LORD? And the Gibeonites said unto him, We will have no silver nor gold of Saul, nor of his house; neither for us shalt thou kill any man in Israel. And he said, What ye shall say, that will I do for you. And they answered the king, The man that consumed us, and that devised against us that we should be destroyed from remaining in any of the coasts of Israel, Let seven men of his sons be delivered unto us, and we will hang them up unto the LORD in Gibeah of Saul, whom the LORD did choose. And the king said, I will give them. (2 Sam. 21:1-6.)

This incident where God held Israel accountable for breaking their promise to this deceitful people was many years after the original promise. Time does not negate our promise. Other examples of promises, some of which spanned multiple generations, include:

- God made seven covenants with man: Adamic (Gen. 3:16-19), Noahic (Gen. 9:11-12), Abrahamic (Gen. 15:18), Palestinian (Deut. 30:1-10), Mosaic (Deut. 4:13, 5:2-3, 9:9), Davidic (2 Sam. 7:8-16), and new covenant (Jer. 31:31-34).
- Amalek – who mistreated Israel in the days of Moses and whom God promised to utterly destroy. Saul was told to destroy them several generations later. His disobedience caused God to dethrone him for not upholding the curse. His disobedience meant that Amalek was still a thorn in Israel's side right up to the time of

Haman. (Exod. 17:8-16; Num. 24:20; Deut. 25:17-19; 1 Sam. 15:2-22, 28:18; 1 Chr. 4:42-43), note Haman was an Agagite, a descendant of Agag, the king of the Amalekites (Est 3:1);
- Abraham and Abimelech (Gen 21:23-24);
- Abraham and his servant, concerning the finding of a wife for Isaac (Gen 24:3-8, 37-41) which we also briefly mentioned;
- Esau and Jacob (Gen. 25:33; Heb. 12:16);
- Jephthah and his daughter (Judg. 11:30-40 already mentioned in an earlier chapter).
- The most fundamental of all human covenants is that of the marriage covenant (Gen. 2:24; Mat. 19:7-9; 1 Cor. 7:10-11; Mal. 2:14-16; Rom. 7:2-3).

The reason why keeping one's word as a Christian is so crucial, is because we are supposed to reflect God's character (Heb. 6:13-20 - which describes the reliability of God's oath, a reflection of His immutable character.) Each time we fail to keep a promise, we tell everyone watching that words do not have meaning and can't be relied upon. This of course cuts to the very heart of the gospel, since if men can't believe us, why should they believe our account of the gospel? Why should they believe that God keeps His word? Time does not negate testimony.

What can we learn from all of this?
1. Discernment and caution are necessary before making a covenant: Joshua and the princes were deceived yet they made a league which they were bound by. Even though the Gibeonites were not the people of God, yet God honoured the league made by Joshua and pun-

ished the Children of Israel in David's time for the sin of Saul, at least two generations after the league was made. The famine was only lifted when the Israelites made the requested restitution, however sometimes there is no appropriate restitution which can be made to remedy the damage. Saul would have known the history of the Gibeonites and while his actions to the uninitiated may have seemed commendable, i.e. destroying those who were not God's, his actions were deplorable because he broke the league made by God's people with them. This is a warning to be careful before covenanting in marriage. If one is deceived into thinking that a potential spouse has a character which they do not have, or if blind to something which later will become an issue, there is no opting out of the covenant (Rom. 7:2-3).

2. Covenanting, promising and making oaths reflects the immutability of God's counsel and thus is very serious when broken since, if such promises are made by God's people, it reflects on God himself (see Heb. 6:16-17).
3. Such binding of ourselves must be made carefully, as demonstrated, because the life of the oath may extend beyond our life time. David suffered because of Saul, yet the promise was made by Joshua.
4. James warns us about oaths. This verse must be taken as a warning rather than a prohibition on oaths because marriage is a covenant sanctioned by God (James 5:12).
5. Does God still chastise for broken oaths today? Even in 1 Cor. 11 members of the local church suffer when not rightly discerning the body and blood of the Lord Jesus Christ. We have no indication that God deals with oaths any different today than He always did and since

His character is immutable and we have the warning of condemnation in James 5:12, we can assume that He still takes them as seriously today as He ever did. After all, as already noted, they reflect on His very own character. Let us, as David did, inquire of the Lord if we notice any seemingly unexplained prolonged trial in our lives. Let us understand too that our word is the most fundamental glue when it comes to relationships.

CHAPTER 10

The Tongue Is A Fire

The fruit of our lips comes from the root of our heart and is the vehicle by which relationships are sustained or destroyed.

Behold, we put bits in the horses' mouths, that they may obey us; and we turn about their whole body. Behold also the ships, which though they be so great, and are driven of fierce winds, yet are they turned about with a very small helm, whithersoever the governor listeth. Even so the tongue is a little member, and boasteth great things. Behold, how great a matter a little fire kindleth! And the tongue is a fire, a world of iniquity: so is the tongue among our members, that it defileth the whole body, and setteth on fire the course of nature; and it is set on fire of hell. For every kind of beasts, and of birds, and of serpents, and of things in the sea, is tamed, and hath been tamed of mankind: But the tongue can no man tame; it is an unruly evil, full of deadly poison. Therewith bless we God, even the Father; and therewith curse we men, which are made after the similitude of God. Out of the same mouth proceedeth blessing and cursing. My brethren, these things ought not so to be. (James 3:3-10.)

God's Word is full of warnings about the fruit of our lips. Let us meditate upon some of these gems.

For my mouth shall speak truth; and wickedness is an abomination to my lips. (Prov. 8:7.)

Set a watch, O LORD, before my mouth; keep the door of my lips. (Psalm 141:3.)

An ungodly man diggeth up evil: and in his lips there is as a burning fire. (Prov. 16:27.)

The lips of the righteous know what is acceptable: but the mouth of the wicked speaketh frowardness. (Prov. 10:32.)

Even a fool, when he holdeth his peace, is counted wise: and he that shutteth his lips is esteemed a man of understanding. (Prov. 17:28.)

The lips of the wise disperse knowledge: but the heart of the foolish doeth not so. (Prov. 15:7.)

Put away from thee a froward mouth, and perverse lips put far from thee. (Prov. 4:24.)

There is gold, and a multitude of rubies: but the lips of knowledge are a precious jewel. (Prov. 20:15.)

The heart of the righteous studieth to answer: but the mouth of the wicked poureth out evil things. (Prov. 15:28.)

The words of a wise man's mouth are gracious; but the lips of a fool will swallow up himself. (Eccl. 10:12.)

A soft answer turneth away wrath: but grievous words stir up anger. (Prov. 15:1.)

Let your speech be alway with grace, seasoned with salt, that ye may know how ye ought to answer every man. (Col. 4:6.)

Keep thy tongue from evil, and thy lips from speaking guile. (Ps. 34:13.)

For he that will love life, and see good days, let him refrain his tongue from evil, and his lips that they speak no guile: (1 Peter 3:10.)

But I say unto you, That every idle word that men shall speak, they shall give account thereof in the day of judgment. (Mat. 12:36.)

Let us summarize some of these thoughts.
1. If we habitually sin with our mouth, we need to examine our heart because our words only reflect what is in our heart!
2. We need to pray for help. Let the words of my mouth, and the meditation of my heart, be acceptable in thy sight, O LORD, my strength, and my redeemer.

3. The tongue is a little member and yet has great power to hurt or to heal.
4. The lips of the righteous know what is appropriate to talk about.
5. An ungodly man digs up evil.
6. Let our words be few because the more we say, the more likely we'll sin.
7. Avoid contention for contention's sake.
8. Learn how to control our tongue.
9. Be purposeful with our words.
10. Every idle word that men shall speak, they shall give account thereof in the day of judgment.

CHAPTER 11

What Is Love?

Though I speak with the tongues of men and of angels, and have not charity, I am become as sounding brass, or a tinkling cymbal. And though I have the gift of prophecy, and understand all mysteries, and all knowledge; and though I have all faith, so that I could remove mountains, and have not charity, I am nothing. And though I bestow all my goods to feed the poor, and though I give my body to be burned, and have not charity, it profiteth me nothing. Charity suffereth long, and is kind; charity envieth not; charity vaunteth not itself, is not puffed up, Doth not behave itself unseemly, seeketh not her own, is not easily provoked, thinketh no evil; Rejoiceth not in iniquity, but rejoiceth in the truth; Beareth all things, believeth all things, hopeth all things, endureth all things. (1 Cor. 13:1-7.)

The Greek language is extremely rich and has multiple words to express the various kinds and aspects of our single word "love". The classical Greek word *Eros* was a term used to describe hot, unendurable desire. Storge was a word used by the Greeks to describe a strong familial love that protects and makes secure. Phileo described the brotherly love of family or friendship. And then there was agape, which was usually used to describe God's most profound and pure love.

While other words for love do appear in Scripture, such as phileo (brotherly love), philandros (the love which a wife has for her husband), philoteknos (love for one's children), and others, the great majority of references to love in the context of person to person or person to God use agape (noun) or agapao (verb). Since this word is used uniquely in the New Testament we must appeal only to scripture for its meaning. An excerpt from Vine's New Testament Dictionary follows:

> "A-1, Verb, 25, agapao and the corresponding noun agape present "the characteristic word of Christianity, and since the Spirit of revelation has used it to express ideas previously unknown, inquiry into its use, whether in Greek literature or in the Septuagint, throws but little light upon its distinctive meaning in the NT. cf. however, Lev. 19:18; Deut. 6:5."

Agape and agapao are used in the NT -
- to describe the attitude of God toward His Son, John 17:26; the human race, generally, John 3:16; Rom 5:8; and to such as believe on the Lord Jesus Christ, particularly, John 14:21;
- to convey His will to His children concerning their attitude one toward another, John 13:34, and toward all men, 1 Thess. 3:12; 1 Cor. 16:14; 2 Peter 1:7;
- to express the essential nature of God, 1 John 4:8.

Christian love has God for its primary object, and expresses itself first of all in implicit obedience to His commandments, John 14:15 21 23; 15:10; 1 John 2:5; 5:3; 2 John 1:6. Self-will, that is, self-pleasing, is the negation of love to God.

All the ordinary words for love express emotion. Agape is different – it has to do with the mind; it is not just an emotion. It is a deliberate principle of mind and a specific decision of the will. This word occurs over 250 times in the NT.

This helps us to understand how the Lord Jesus can say that we are to love the Lord with all our hearts etc. (Mat. 22:37). Can love be commanded? Can an emotion be called forth from a cold heart? Hardly. But a command from the Lord Jesus to love God (agapao) is a command to obey, and that is something which a believer is able to do, for "the love of God is shed abroad in his heart" (Rom. 5:5.)

When couples are in marital distress, if only the love of God flooded their hearts they would know that they are to love each other, even if they do not feel it. For love is commitment; it means "I will do all I can to make life comfortable for my spouse"; it means "I will only seek the best for my spouse." And when the mind and will decide on that course, agape love is being expressed. If the members of the body of Christ in the local church understood this agape, we would not be so quick to leave when we disagree or have to work through issues arising from personality conflicts.

(In the following two lists, definitions in parentheses are literal translations from the Greek word or concept used.)

Agape Love:
- is patient – shows self-restraint when provoked, does not hastily retaliate;
- is kind - useful, gracious, beneficial;
- rejoices with the truth (God's Word is Truth John 17:17);
- bears all things - covers and protects like a roof covers a house to protect it from storms. It does not mean that love bears all sin in the way that a doormat passively takes the feet of its users;
- believes all things (which God has revealed, i.e. truth);
- hopes all things (It is optimistic rather than pessimistic because God is in control) (Col. 1:27);
- endures all things (doesn't quit);
- never fails (It can withstand anything as its source is God), (1 Cor. 13:4-8.);
- is an act of the will (Mark 12:30; 1 Thes. 1:3; Heb. 6:10, 10:24; 1 John 3:18);
- is to be initiated without expectation of reciprocation (Luke 6:32);
- is the mark of the Lord's disciples recognised by all men (John 13:35; 1 John 5:2);
- is obedience to the Lord's commandments (John 14:15, 21; 1 John 2:5; 2 John 1:6);
- clings to that which is good (Rom. 12:9);
- treats others more honourably than self (Rom. 12:10);
- sums up the whole law (Rom. 13:9);
- is a fruit of the Spirit (Gal. 5:22).

Agape Love is not:
- Nice sounding words without the action to back them up (1 Cor. 13:1; Ps. 55:21; Pr. 17:6, 23:6-7, 26:23-26);
- sacrificial giving (1 Cor. 13:3), one can sacrificially give and yet not love;
- envious - does not resent the blessings, successes, or well-being of others;
- self-exalting – engage in self-promotion;
- pompous – demonstrate an inflated ego;
- indecent - will never make inappropriate demands of others, i.e. ask another to disobey God;
- self-seeking - is not so consumed with its own interests that it cannot show concern for the needs and interests of others;
- easily provoked – is not easily driven to irritation or sharpness of spirit;
- an accumulator of past evils - one who keeps records of wrongs with the intent of someday getting even;
- delighted by iniquity - does not find delight in anything God says is wrong. Neither does it take secret satisfaction in the moral failures of others (1 Cor. 13:4-7; Rom. 12:9);
- hypocritical – holds a higher standard for others than themselves (Rom. 12:9);

The agape love which we are commanded to have is always in conjunction with the discernment of good and evil. If we have God's agape love in us then we will be obedient to Him, that is, we will abhor what He designates as evil and cling to what He says is good. We cannot have the agape love of God in us if we consider what He deems evil to be good nor what He deems good to be evil (Isa. 5:20). It is the obedience to God's commandments that determines if we have agape love in us and not whether we hold to the opinions of others, especially those of the world (who brand us as unloving). We cannot have the agape love of God in us if we love the world or the things herein! (1 John 2:15).

While we may feel *phileo* or other forms of love for one-another, we are commanded to have agape. We are not being unloving if we expose error. We are not being unloving if we correct a brother or sister in error. We are not unloving if we put a brother or sister who continues in sin out of fellowship (1 Cor. 5:11-12). We are not unloving if we separate ourselves from worldly practises, and if need be, professing Christians who are worldly. (Eph. 5:9-11; Rom. 16:17-18; 2 Cor. 6:17; Luke 6:22; 2 John 1:9-11; 1 Thes. 5:22; Mat. 18:15-17). We must always remember that the command to love God with our complete being comes before the command to love our neighbour as our self. Thus, loving God should dictate how we express love for our neighbour. (Mark 12:30-33.)

Agape love is an act of the will and something we should be actively demonstrating to all, especially other believers (Gal. 6:10). Let us continually examine how we love others by comparing our actions and attitudes with the scriptural definition of agape love. This final passage really sums up why our right expression of God's agape love is so crucial. Just like keeping our word reflects on the very nature of Christ, after whom Christians are named (Acts 11:26; 2 Tim. 2:19), so too, our love for one another should be a reflection of God's love and not the world's perverted definition.

In this was manifested the love of God toward us, because that God sent his only begotten Son into the world, that we might live through him. Herein is love, not that we loved God, but that he loved us, and sent his Son to be the propitiation for our sins. Beloved, if God so loved us, we ought also to love one another. (1 John 4:9-11.)

After considering this most profound relationship glue, it is no wonder the apostle Paul concluded that when all else fails, "The greatest of these is love!" (1 Cor. 13:13.)

CHAPTER 12

Who Is The Greatest?

Sibling rivalry in the family and in the household of faith causes untold damage to relationships. The Lord Jesus made it abundantly clear that those who focus on being the greatest, have the completely opposite mindset to what they ought to have. He told His disciples that if they wanted to be the greatest, they had to learn to be the greatest servant. They had to be as humble as an infant. Interestingly, this again is best learned in the home as parents receive totally dependent infants, and raise them to adulthood.

> At the same time came the disciples unto Jesus, saying, Who is the greatest in the kingdom of heaven? And Jesus called a little child unto him, and set him in the midst of them, And said, Verily I say unto you, Except ye be converted, and become as little children, ye shall not enter into the kingdom of heaven. Whosoever therefore shall humble himself as this little child, the same is greatest in the kingdom of heaven. And whoso shall receive one such little child in my name receiveth me. But whoso shall offend one of these little ones which believe in me, it were better for

him that a millstone were hanged about his neck, and that he were drowned in the depth of the sea. (Mat. 18:1-6.)

The Lord Jesus again addresses the same issue of wanting to be the greatest when the apostles James and John ask Him to sit at His right and left hand in His kingdom. The Lord's response was in the form of a question to them, could they drink of His cup of suffering?

> And James and John, the sons of Zebedee, come unto him, saying, Master, we would that thou shouldest do for us whatsoever we shall desire. And he said unto them, What would ye that I should do for you? They said unto him, Grant unto us that we may sit, one on thy right hand, and the other on thy left hand, in thy glory. But Jesus said unto them, Ye know not what ye ask: can ye drink of the cup that I drink of? and be baptized with the baptism that I am baptized with? And they said unto him, We can. And Jesus said unto them, Ye shall indeed drink of the cup that I drink of; and with the baptism that I am baptized withal shall ye be baptized: But to sit on my right hand and on my left hand is not mine to give; but it shall be given to them for whom it is prepared. And when the ten heard it, they began to be much displeased with James and John. But Jesus called them to him, and saith unto them, Ye know that they which are accounted to rule over the Gentiles exercise lordship over them; and their great ones exercise authority upon them. But so shall it not be among you: but whosoever will be great among you, shall be your minister: And whosoever of you will be the chiefest, shall be servant of all. For even the Son of man came not to be ministered unto, but

to minister, and to give his life a ransom for many. (Mark 10:35-45.)

While we briefly mentioned the below passage in our chapter on the husband, it is worth reiterating here.

> Now before the feast of the passover, when Jesus knew that his hour was come that he should depart out of this world unto the Father, having loved his own which were in the world, he loved them unto the end. And supper being ended, the devil having now put into the heart of Judas Iscariot, Simon's son, to betray him; Jesus knowing that the Father had given all things into his hands, and that he was come from God, and went to God; He riseth from supper, and laid aside his garments; and took a towel, and girded himself. After that he poureth water into a basin, and began to wash the disciples' feet, and to wipe them with the towel wherewith he was girded. ... So after he had washed their feet, and had taken his garments, and was set down again, he said unto them, Know ye what I have done to you? Ye call me Master and Lord: and ye say well; for so I am. If I then, your Lord and Master, have washed your feet; ye also ought to wash one another's feet. For I have given you an example, that ye should do as I have done to you. Verily, verily, I say unto you, The servant is not greater than his lord; neither he that is sent greater than he that sent him. If ye know these things, happy are ye if ye do them. (John 13:1-5, 12-17.)

In today's modern church, where many preach the prosperity gospel, this is a hard truth to swallow. The Christian life is not about material blessing, nor about being the centre of the universe, but worshipping the one who is. It is about learning to be a disciple of one who was spat upon, mocked, scourged, and ultimately crucified, even though He only went about doing good (Acts 10:38). On one occasion, He even asked, "For which good work do you seek to stone me?" (John 10:32). He so aptly reminds us that a mature disciple is one who is like his master, i.e. a servant whose good works are not dependent upon the treatment received of others.

> The disciple is not above his master: but every one that is perfect shall be as his master. (Luke 6:40.)

> For, brethren, ye have been called unto liberty; only use not liberty for an occasion to the flesh, but by love serve one another. (Gal. 5:13.)

> Likewise, ye younger, submit yourselves unto the elder. Yea, all of you be subject one to another, and be clothed with humility: for God resisteth the proud, and giveth grace to the humble. (1 Peter 5:5.)

We must train our children from very young to have a servant attitude. This of course must be done by exemplifying a servant attitude ourselves. The most obvious way is in how we treat our wife. We can't expect our boys to treat their sisters with respect when they are older if we do not train them from young that they are their sister's protectors. We can't expect our girls to submit to a husband if we do not train them to respect their brothers and come under the authority of their father. While courtesy is to be extended to all, training boys to respect girls is different to training girls to respect boys. For example, you may train your boys to open doors for their mother and sisters, while training girls to serve their brothers at the table. We must encourage the older children to look after the younger children, perhaps helping them to learn their chores or supervising them as they do their daily tasks. We must train the younger children to submit to the elder children. Being a servant does not come naturally to the self-centred sinful human so it is something we must constantly reinforce. Let us finish this chapter with one last self-explanatory parable spoken by the Lord Jesus.

> And he put forth a parable to those which were bidden, when he marked how they chose out the chief rooms; saying unto them. When thou art bidden of any man to a wedding, sit not down in the highest room; lest a more honourable man than thou be bidden of him; And he that bade thee and him come and say to thee, Give this man place; and thou begin with shame to take the lowest room. But when thou art bidden, go and sit down in the lowest room; that when he that bade thee cometh, he may say unto thee, Friend, go up higher: then shalt thou have worship in the presence of them that sit at meat with thee. For whosoever exalteth himself shall be abased; and he that humbleth himself shall be exalted. Then said he also to him that bade him, When thou makest a dinner or a supper, call not thy friends, nor thy brethren, neither thy kinsmen, nor thy rich neighbours; lest they also bid thee again, and a recompence be made thee. But when thou makest a feast, call the poor, the maimed, the lame, the blind: And thou shalt be blessed; for they cannot recompense thee: for thou shalt be recompensed at the resurrection of the just. (Luke 14:7-14.)

CHAPTER 13

Family Worship And Discipleship

You may ask what family worship has to do with relationships in the family and in the church. By the end of this chapter I hope you will see.

What is worship? Worship means to show adoration, reverence, respect and dependence upon God, that is, to recognize His worth-ship, not just as the Almighty being, but also for every word, precept, command, principle or judgment spoken by Him. The New Testament word for worship expresses the humble devotion of a dog licking its master's hand. We often associate worship with the externals of singing or prostration, yet these externals are hollow rituals if in action we show His Word to be worthless.

> Wherefore the Lord said, Forasmuch as this people draw near me with their mouth, and with their lips do honour me, but have removed their heart far from me, and their fear toward me is taught by the precept of men: (Isa. 29:13.)

> But the hour cometh, and now is, when the true worshippers shall worship the Father in spirit and in truth: for the Father seeketh such to worship him. God is a Spirit: and they that worship him must worship him in spirit and in truth. (John 4:23-24.)

If worship was so common, surely the Father would not have to seek true worshipers as these verses suggest. We need to get away from the stereotypical view that worship is something we turn on and off. We all know the feeling, you walk in to an emotion charged church meeting after having a fight at home and go straight into singing emotional songs. We switch into and out of worship mode like the way we separate secular and sacred parts of our lives. This is not worship. There should be no distinction between secular and sacred, nor between worship and non-worship. Our entire lives are to be lived under the Lordship of Christ and in an attitude of worship.

> I beseech you therefore, brethren, by the mercies of God, that ye present your bodies a living sacrifice, holy, acceptable unto God, which is your reasonable service. And be not conformed to this world: but be ye transformed by the renewing of your mind, that ye may prove what is that good, and acceptable, and perfect, will of God. (Rom. 12:1-2.)

Some translations render the last two words of Romans 12:1 as reasonable worship. We see from these verses that worship begins with the presentation or yielding of our bodies to God as living sacrifices. This presentation is our reasonable or logical requirement of worship or service. (cf. Dan 3:28). Anything less than presenting our bodies to God is not reasonable or logical worship. That is, it is not just in the heart and mind that worship occurs, but it is consecrating our entire being as the temple of the Holy Spirit. This involves being transformed by the renewing of our mind that we may be conformed to the likeness of the Lord Jesus Christ. We cannot be conformed to the Lord's likeness, nor know the will of God for our lives, without the renewal of our mind. More often than not, our minds are saturated from infancy with worldly philosophies which are at enmity with God and it takes an incredible amount of discipline and honest searching of the Scriptures to renew our minds. Presenting our bodies is not popular, it actually requires that we consider everything our bodies are involved in in light of God's searching light of Scripture. This involves diet, dress, language, thought, action, attitude, response, expression.

> If ye love me, keep my commandments. (John 14:15.)

Worship is thus our demonstration of love for God by our willing and humble obedience to Him. It begins with what we choose to fill our mind with.

> The wicked, through the pride of his countenance, will not seek after God: God is not in all his thoughts. (Ps. 10:4.)

Compare this to the Christian who, like David, should have God in all of our thoughts.

I have set the LORD always before me: because he is at my right hand, I shall not be moved. (Ps. 16:8.)

O how I love thy law! It is my meditation all the day. (Ps. 119:97.)

Mine eyes prevent the night watches, that I might meditate in thy word. (Ps. 119:148.)

Family worship thus begins by a conscious decision to nurture a culture of God's worth-ship in our homes, whether we live alone, whether we are married with no children, or whether we have many children. If we have children, nurturing this culture of worth-ship must begin while our children are very young, little by little, line upon line (Isa. 28:9-10; 2 Tim. 3:15.) Worship is the demonstrating of His worth-ship by our non-conformance to the world and our conformance to the likeness of His Son. It is the trust in and valuing of God's entire written revelation - precepts, principles, patterns, statutes and commands, appropriately applied to our life. Singing and adoration in prayer are simply outward manifestations, the overflowing of a heart that is already demonstrating God's worth-ship, that loves God, longs to be like Him and longs to please Him. It is a diligent, conscious effort to be obedient. It is not some formal stale or stifling list of things we must do.

Family worship is thus not just Bible memorization, study, singing and praying, though these are obviously essential, but is about nurturing a culture in our homes where

God is in all our thoughts. May I encourage us all to remember that non-conformance to the world doesn't just mean not watching the same movies or doing what the world does, it is even in our diet, dress and speech. Worth-ship is moving in the direction of total conformance, both inward and outward.

We have heard a lot about alcohol abuse over the history of the church but how many sermons have you heard on gluttony in recent years? What about looking after the temple of the Holy Spirit? What about hospitality? What about modesty?

Our speech should be different to the world, filled with grace, seasoned with salt (Col. 4:6). How many Christians do you know who have adopted the world's speech culture, using the word wicked to mean exciting or good?

> Woe unto them that call evil good, and good evil; that put darkness for light, and light for darkness; that put bitter for sweet, and sweet for bitter! (Is. 5:20.)

Our dress should be distinct, remember, it is an abomination to God for a woman to wear a man's clothing and vice versa

> The woman shall not wear that which pertaineth unto a man, neither shall a man put on a woman's garment: for all that do so are abomination unto the LORD thy God. (Deu. 22:5.)

> In like manner also, that women adorn themselves in modest apparel, with shamefacedness and sobriety; not with broided hair, or gold, or pearls, or costly array; But (which becometh women professing godliness) with good works. (1 Tim. 2:9-10.)

It is also a shame for a man to grow his hair long or for a woman to be shorn.

> Doth not even nature itself teach you, that, if a man have long hair, it is a shame unto him? But if a woman have long hair, it is a glory to her: for her hair is given her for a covering. (1 Cor. 11:14-15.)

Perhaps in the church we don't see too many men wearing dresses, though we see increasing numbers growing their hair long. We do however see plenty of women wearing immodest clothing or men's clothing. One may argue that our culture no longer dresses as they did 400 years ago. Perhaps, but our culture also thinks that homosexuality and fornication are OK and that traditional marriage is old fashioned. It is a sobering lesson to consider what was worn at the height of Christian reformation, when Christians roamed the earth and the Bible was brought to bear upon culture. Women, before feminism and a mass exodus from the home, wore dresses and grew their hair long while men wore the pants and cut their hair short. Women's and men's clothes should be modest and distinct. Adam and Eve sought to cover as much of their nakedness as possible yet we, even as Christians, often see how far we can go in dressing like the immodest, androgynous culture around us which seeks to reveal as much as possible, and remove any distinction between the clothing worn by men and women. This is only a recent change.

Culture is religion externalized, what we wear sends a message just as how we talk sends a message, often even more than what we actually say. What you wear reflects the values you want communicated to others. We often hear that man looks upon the outward appearance, but God sees the heart (1 Sam 16:7). This is true, but what is in the heart must be manifest outwardly. Also, we are supposed to be in the world but not of it. We are not to be conformed to the world but transformed by the renewing of our mind. Have we renewed our mind on these issues? Remember, worship is about the estimation of God's work and Word in our lives. This is not about legalism. Both internals and externals matter according to Romans 12:1-2.

> Woe unto you, scribes and Pharisees, hypocrites! for ye pay tithe of mint and anise and cummin, and have omitted the weightier matters of the law, judgment, mercy, and faith: these ought ye to have done, and not to leave the other undone. (Mat. 23:23.)

Note the final words of the previous verse, "these ought ye to have done, and not to leave the other undone." That is, internals and externals both matter. It is when we have the externals without the internals that we have hypocrisy. It is important to state that we do not do such works of worship to get saved, but we worship God through our works once we have been saved (Eph. 2:10; James 2:18). Worship is for those who have already trusted the complete work of the Lord Jesus Christ upon the cross for their personal sin, nothing we can do can earn this salvation (Eph. 2:8-9; Rom. 6:23; John 3:16). Of course we must still teach our children the ways of the Lord, even before they profess faith in Christ (Eph. 6:4). Again, the works of obedience that we do are because we are saved, not in order to be saved.

Once we understand that worship is about worth-ship, and family worship is about God's worth-ship in our home lives, we can begin to think about the ways this worship is expressed. Our attitudes even to these externals just mentioned are often formed in the home by what we allow or disallow, the appetites we encourage, and the culture we nurture in our homes.

> Hear, O Israel: The LORD our God is one LORD: And thou shalt love the LORD thy God with all thine heart, and with all thy soul, and with all thy might. And these words, which I command thee this day, shall be in thine heart: And thou shalt teach them diligently unto thy children, and shalt talk of them when thou sittest in thine house, and when thou walkest by the way, and when thou liest down, and when thou risest up. And thou shalt bind them for a sign upon thine hand, and they shall be as frontlets between thine eyes. And thou shalt write them upon the posts of thy house, and on thy gates. (Deu. 6:4-8.)

Family worship has its expression in every area of our home lives. Note the example of family worship given to

Israel which we'd do well to follow, even in the church age. Remember, Israel was to be a light to the nations, teaching the rest of the World the goodness and sensibility of God's ways (Deut. 4:5-10). Deuteronomy 6 begins by reiterating the first commandment to love God with our heart, mind, soul and strength and then goes on to describe when and how this love and worship is to be expressed. The when includes when we sit in our house (at meal time), when we walk together (as we work and interact together), when we retire for the evening, and when we first wake. Finally it has outward expression, on our doorposts and gates, i.e. publically visible to the outside community.

When thou sittest in thine house:
When we sit in our homes around the table, we are to read, study and discuss the Word of God. Even if you have no children, we see this alluded to by the apostle Paul who tells women to ask their own husbands at home if they want to learn something about the Word of God (1 Cor. 14:35). Throughout history, that is up until recently, the table has been the centre of fellowship and worship in the home (Ps. 128:3). As we renew our minds and cast off the individualistic fast food culture, we need to restore this practice in our homes. As you sit at meal times, at least one meal time a day, more if you are able, take time to read, memorize, pray, discuss and even sing together. As fathers, we should be able to pick up our Bible and teach our family from basically any passage. We are to address the issues of the day by bringing the Word of God to bear upon our culture. The Bible is relevant for all time and every culture. The gospel is far more than a ticket to heaven, it is a transforming power which transforms culture through transformed families

made up of transformed individuals. As we study the Scriptures, there are many ways we must do it. We can obviously learn history and prophesy, but this is too often taught in such a way that it is detached from the present reality. More than just a religious textbook for the past or future, we must study how to think and behave. We must also teach how to discern godly character by studying the many examples of good and bad characters throughout Scripture and God's dealings with them. We want our children to be able to recognize wise friends, wise work partners and of course godly and wise spouses. Remember, worship is worth-ship, that is, magnifying the worth of God in our living of life. Fathers, it is our job to set the example in nurturing this attitude of family worship in our homes. Note the decision and proclamation by Joshua, "... as for me and my house, we will serve the LORD." (Josh. 24:15b)

Many fathers use catechisms to teach their families. These and other books and tools may be useful occasionally but I'd encourage you to go straight to the Word of God. Too often fathers go no deeper than reading "Everyday with Jesus" or other such daily readings. These have their uses but I'd strongly encourage you to wean yourself from these and go deeper and teach your family what God is teaching you through your own study of the Scriptures rather than someone else's meditations. As a church we've become too dependent on others doing the hard work of study rather than delving into the Word of God ourselves and by prayer and petition learning the heart and will of God. If we don't read the Scriptures ourselves, we'll just be clones of others, regurgitating exactly what they thought without knowing why we believe what we believe. Get the Word of God firsthand, not second-hand. If our family worship is strong, it makes our coming together as a church, the body of believers, much more fruitful, and, removes the constant burden of reiterating the first principles of the gospel to those who should, through family worship, have progressed from these first principles. For too long we have tolerated a spoon feeding culture of men who should take the burden of responsibility back from the church into their family as God intended. We need to truly have a New Testament view of the church, rather than a view based upon the traditions of men. The New Testament church was a body of believers who enjoyed mutual fellowship and worshipped together, not constant spoon feeding from one pastor. This is why 1 Cor. 14:26-35 is so clear about each man coming prepared to give.

> For when for the time ye ought to be teachers, ye have need that one teach you again which be the first principles of the oracles of God; and are become such as have need of milk, and not of strong meat. For every one that useth milk is unskilful in the word of righteousness: for he is a babe. But strong meat belongeth to them that are of full age, even those who by reason of use have their senses exercised to discern both good and evil. Therefore leaving the principles of the doctrine of Christ, let us go on unto perfection; not laying again the foundation of repentance from dead works, and of faith toward God, Of the doctrine of baptisms, and of laying on of hands, and of resurrection of the dead, and of eternal judgment. (Heb. 5:12-6:2.)

Our church order is an extension of our family worship. If we are disorderly and irreverent in our family worship, this irreverence will be evident in our church meetings. If our family relationships are shallow, egalitarian and selfish, so too this will be reflected in the church.

> God is greatly to be feared in the assembly of the saints, and to be had in reverence of all them that are about him. (Ps. 89:7.)

When thou walkest by the way:
It is important to realise that work is also worship. Work which demonstrates God's worth-ship through reflecting His character in diligence, perseverance, honesty and integrity, applying the principles of His Word to the way we do business (Rom. 12:11). I've heard of men who simply stroll the beach meditating all day every day, thinking they're spiritual. God said that if a man doesn't work, neither shall he eat. The apostle Paul also said that true spirituality is recognizing that what he taught was the commandment of God and to be obeyed, not simply meditated upon.

> If any man think himself to be a prophet, or spiritual, let him acknowledge that the things that I write unto you are the commandments of the Lord. (1 Cor. 14:37.)

> For even when we were with you, this we commanded you, that if any would not work, neither should he eat. (2 Thes. 3:10.)

We are worshipping when we work to provide for our families and for the provision of the saints. It is worship because God commands men to work. This doesn't mean that's all we do. We must not fall into the trap of only working and not taking the Lord's day off for rest and corporate worship in the assembly of believers.

> But if any provide not for his own, and specially for those of his own house, he hath denied the faith, and is worse than an infidel. (1 Tim. 5:8.)

Women too work in the home. I don't like the term "stay at home mum", it implies mothers do not work. They are the busiest people I know, especially if they educate their children according to the Scriptural pattern of home based discipleship. Don't underestimate work as worship.

> I will therefore that the younger women marry, bear children, guide the house, give none occasion to the adversary to speak reproachfully. (1 Tim. 5:14.)

> That they may teach the young women to be sober, to love their husbands, to love their children, To be discreet, chaste, keepers at home, good, obedient to their own husbands, that the word of God be not blasphemed. (Titus 2:4-5.)

Don't get caught in the trap of sacrifice in disobedience. Too often as Christians we would rather make sacrifice to serve the Lord rather than obey His clear commands (1

Sam. 15:22). Our worship is negated by disobedience since disobedience does not demonstrate God's worth-ship but that God's Word is worthless. I can't stress this enough. Look around you, the truth of Isaiah 3:12 is plainly evident in our society and the church needs to recover these truths.

> As for my people, children are their oppressors, and women rule over them. O my people, they which lead thee cause thee to err, and destroy the way of thy paths. (Isa. 3:12.)

This starts in the home through our family worth-ship by respecting and teaching, rather than arguing away, the roles and appropriate work of men and women ordained by God. Work is worship. So our work must be the work determined by God if it is to be acceptable worship.

When thou liest down, and when thou risest up:
When we retire for the evening and when we first wake, God should be in our thoughts. Often we are encouraged to have a quiet time in the morning, presumably because the Lord Jesus spent time with His father before daylight (Mark 1:35). This is of course a good practise, but it almost implies that once it is over, the rest of the day is ours. Let us remember our starting Psalm, 10:4, and the verses from Psalm 119. God is to be in all our thoughts, and in our thoughts continually. There is no such thing as "me" time in the Christian life.

> What? know ye not that your body is the temple of the Holy Ghost which is in you, which ye have of

God, and ye are not your own? For ye are bought with a price: therefore glorify God in your body, and in your spirit, which are God's. (1 Cor. 6:19-20.)

Finally, Deuteronomy 6:8-9 makes it clear that our family worship is to be public. This simply means that what we teach and practice in the home is to be reflected in our public testimony.

And thou shalt bind them for a sign upon thine hand, and they shall be as frontlets between thine eyes. And thou shalt write them upon the posts of thy house, and on thy gates. (Deu. 6:9.)

Summary:
- Works of worship do not save us but are performed because we are saved.
- Worship is showing God's worth-ship by the way we live.
- God is to be in all our thoughts.
- We not only demonstrate worship through Bible study, prayer and singing, but through obedience which shows that we hold His Word in the highest esteem.
- Worship begins by yielding our bodies to God as living sacrifices, it is not just in the mind and heart.
- Family Worship is nurturing a culture of God's worth-ship in our home through teaching and applying God's Word to every aspect of our lives: dress, diet, attitude, action, response, expression, etc. Internals must become externals.

- The family table is the centre of our fellowship and should habitually incorporate Bible study, memorization, discussion, prayer and singing.
- Work in our appropriate sphere is acceptable worship.
- Our attitude of worship begins when we rise up and doesn't stop until we sleep.
- Our worship is to be evident to those outside.

Family worship has everything to do with Biblical relationships because it is the foundation of all relationships. Worship reminds us of our subjection to the head of every man, Christ. If we are humbly walking with our God (Micah 6:8), we will be less likely to abuse our power as fathers. If the relationship under God is right, the flow on effect will be felt in the rest of the family. If family worship is established, worship on the Lord's day, in the public assembly of believers will be a natural consequence, not a contrived performance. If you understand your position under God, you will recognize the dignity of human life. You will recognize His creation order. You will love your neighbour as yourself. A constant attitude of worship in the family will keep our hearts sensitive to the conviction of sin and help us to refocus on what needs correction in our family life. This is why the apostle Paul told Timothy that if one cannot rule his own household well, how can he rule the church of God (1 Tim. 3:5). As we practice Deuteronomy 6 in our homes, the natural consequence of such discipleship will be strong relationships which will overflow into the church and into the wider community.

Chapter 14

What We Do In Private

But the children of Israel committed a trespass in the accursed thing: for Achan, the son of Carmi, the son of Zabdi, the son of Zerah, of the tribe of Judah, took of the accursed thing: and the anger of the LORD was kindled against the children of Israel. ... And Joshua rent his clothes, and fell to the earth upon his face before the ark of the LORD until the eventide, he and the elders of Israel, and put dust upon their heads. And Joshua said, Alas, O Lord GOD, wherefore hast thou at all brought this people over Jordan, to deliver us into the hand of the Amorites, to destroy us? would to God we had been content, and dwelt on the other side Jordan! ... And the LORD said unto Joshua, Get thee up; wherefore liest thou thus upon thy face? Israel hath sinned, and they have also transgressed my covenant which I commanded them: for they have even taken of the accursed thing, and have also stolen, and dissembled also, and they have put it even among their own stuff. (Joshua 7:1, 6-7, 10-11.)

When we suffer through trial, our first reaction is often to blame God rather than search our sinful heart. We question His promises, question His perfect character, focus on anything but our own sin and the possibility that He may be chastening us.

It is important to understand that God's fellowship and provision was withheld from the congregation of Israel until one family's sin was made right. This is very serious. Sin in our midst makes a mockery of God's promises, purposes and plans for the body of believers whether it be the camp of the children of Israel or the assembly of believers today.

> Wherefore whosoever shall eat this bread, and drink this cup of the Lord, unworthily, shall be guilty of the body and blood of the Lord. But let a man examine himself, and so let him eat of that bread, and drink of that cup. For he that eateth and drinketh unworthily, eateth and drinketh damnation to himself, not discerning the Lord's body. For this cause many are weak and sickly among you, and many sleep. For if we would judge ourselves, we should not be judged. But when we are judged, we are chastened of the Lord, that we should not be condemned with the world. (1 Cor. 11:27-32.)

Because God doesn't strike us dead like Ananias and Sapphira (Acts 5), we are not as careful to avoid sin. Because the consequence of our sin does not generally bring the immediate wrath of God, we aren't so careful to ensure our assembly is cleansed from accursed things.

> If we say that we have fellowship with him, and walk in darkness, we lie, and do not the truth: But if we walk in the light, as he is in the light, we have fellowship one with another, and the blood of Jesus Christ his Son cleanseth us from all sin. If we say that we have no sin, we deceive ourselves, and the truth is not in us. If we confess our sins, he is faithful and just to forgive us our sins, and to cleanse us from all unrighteousness. (1 John 1:6-9.)

Israel did not know about Achan's sin. All they knew was defeat. Even Joshua their leader did not know about Achan's sin until the Lord told him about it. While the apostasy of this day is one reason for the lack of strong churches, I strongly suggest that the main reason is hidden sins in our personal lives. The elders may not know about them, the masses may not know about them, but each individual who harbours an accursed thing under their tent knows about it and it causes the breaking of true fellowship amongst believers and causes an assembly to be ineffectual in its witness and testimony. Some of the accursed things we harbour under our tents may include:

- Bitterness - so often, disputes amongst brethren are not dealt with in a scriptural manner. Undercurrents and friction are felt and never addressed. (Mat. 5:23-24.)
- Complacency - it is the duty of the whole body to fulfil their role in the assembly. Too often, too much is left to the wrong people in the wrong season of their lives. Assemblies disintegrate because the youth spend time in leisure when they could be helping the elderly or

young families. Older people retire from their role shepherding the young and feeding the lambs when they retire from their secular jobs. Families are often left to bear the load of hospitality when they still have very young children, resulting in burn-out. (1 Cor. 13:14-19.)
- Self –righteousness - 1 John 1:10.)

Many other accursed things are often hidden in the tabernacles of our hearts: pride, covetousness, idolatry, immorality, etc. Let us all remember that Achan's sin was initially only known by him and his family yet the whole congregation suffered.

Reading 1 Cor. 11:29 in parallel with the account of Achan, we see that Achan brought upon himself damnation not discerning or considering the congregation. So too, sin in a believer's life if not dealt with causes him to partake of the bread and cup unworthily bringing damnation to himself, not considering the Lord's body, that is, not only Christ's physical body, but the assembly which is Christ's spiritual body. We each need to honestly and humbly deal with personal sin because it can negatively impact upon the fellowship, and thus relationships, within the assembly.

Chapter 15

Dealing With Conflict

Conflict
(From More than Meets The Eye, Copyright 2015 by Joseph Stephen)

When the pressure explodes and the Shrapnel flies,
We react in defence to our further demise.
Rather than dealing with a problem's real source,
We try in vain to stave off the force.
It happens to often, we don't seem to learn,
The heat from explosion is certain to burn.
There are signs of the buildup which often forewarn,
So alleviate pressure before the storm.
The extent of the damage, time will reveal,
And the scars from such conflict take longer to heal.
Be sensitive and vigilant to the needs of your wife,
To avoid the pain of acrimonious strife.

Whether it be strife in the home, or strife in the house of God, we will deal with strife sometime in our journey.

> Although affliction cometh not forth of the dust, neither doth trouble spring out of the ground; Yet man is born unto trouble, as the sparks fly upward. (Job 5:6-7.)

There are three ways we can deal with strife, and as we shall see, there is a time for each of these approaches. We can capitulate, we can contend, or we can contribute nothing, i.e. remain silent.

> And when they were come to Capernaum, they that received tribute money came to Peter, and said, Doth not your master pay tribute? He saith, Yes. And when he was come into the house, Jesus prevented him, saying, What thinkest thou, Simon? of whom do the kings of the earth take custom or tribute? of their own children, or of strangers? Peter saith unto him, Of strangers. Jesus saith unto him, Then are the children free. Notwithstanding, lest we should offend them, go thou to the sea, and cast an hook, and take up the fish that first cometh up; and when thou hast opened his mouth, thou shalt find a piece of money: that take, and give unto them for me and thee. (Mat. 17:24-27.)

This passage, in the context of our current subject, demonstrates that there are times when we should simply capitulate rather than push our point and demand our rights. The rulers who demanded this temple tax did not recognize the Lord Jesus as a citizen. They had no right to demand of Peter or the Lord, yet the Lord Jesus complied to avoid offence.

> And the Jews' passover was at hand, and Jesus went up to Jerusalem. And found in the temple those that sold oxen and sheep and doves, and the changers of money sitting: And when he had made a scourge of small cords, he drove them all out of the temple, and the sheep, and the oxen; and poured out the changers' money, and overthrew the tables; And said unto them that sold doves, Take these things hence; make not my Father's house an house of merchandise. And his disciples remembered that it was written, The zeal of thine house hath eaten me up. (John 2:13-17.)

In this second instance, the Lord Jesus contended for the truth with anger, driving out the money changers and overturning their tables.

> And Jesus stood before the governor: and the governor asked him, saying, Art thou the King of the Jews? And Jesus said unto him, Thou sayest. And when he was accused of the chief priests and elders, he answered nothing. (Mat. 27:11-12.)

> He was oppressed, and he was afflicted, yet he opened not his mouth: he is brought as a lamb to the slaughter, and as a sheep before her shearers is dumb, so he openeth not his mouth. (Isa. 53:7.)

In this third instance, incredibly, the Lord Jesus remained completely silent. When examining the instances of each kind of response in the Word of God, I believe we can come to some guiding principles as to how and when to respond in each way.

When it comes to defending the Word of God and the truth, we must earnestly contend (Jude 1:3; Acts 5:29). When it comes to laws, traditions or preferences of man, so long as they do not violate the Word of God, we should capitulate for the sake of peace (Mat. 5:9; Rom. 14:19). When it comes to a situation where our opponent is unlikely to be swayed by our input, contributing nothing is the appropriate response. Different kinds of strife have different levels of consequences. Unless one is defending the truth of God, the overriding principle given by the Lord Jesus was to be a peacemaker. The Apostle Paul echoes this.

> I therefore, the prisoner of the Lord, beseech you that ye walk worthy of the vocation wherewith ye are called, With all lowliness and meekness, with longsuffering, forbearing one another in love; endeavouring to keep the unity of the Spirit in the bond of peace. (Eph. 4:1-3.)

> If it be possible, as much as lieth in you, live peaceably with all men. (Rom. 12:18.)

While this is written to the church, the Lord Jesus made a similar observation which suggests the principle is even more poignant in the family.

> But he, knowing their thoughts, said unto them, Every kingdom divided against itself is brought

to desolation; and a house divided against a house falleth. (Luke 11:17.)

If King Solomon wrote the following about neighbours, how much truer is it within the home and church, especially in light of the prior verse?

Devise not evil against thy neighbour, seeing he dwelleth securely by thee. (Prov. 3:29.)

Be not a witness against thy neighbour without cause; and deceive not with thy lips. Say not, I will do so to him as he hath done to me: I will render to the man according to his work. (Prov. 24:28-29.)

Go not forth hastily to strive, lest thou know not what to do in the end thereof, when thy neighbour hath put thee to shame. (Prov. 25:8.)

Debate thy cause with thy neighbour himself; and discover not a secret to another: (Prov. 25:9.)

Even a fool, when he holdeth his peace, is counted wise: and he that shutteth his lips is esteemed a man of understanding. (Prov. 17:28.)

Since marriage is until death, we would be extremely wise to avoid strife in the family as much as absolutely possible. Except when it comes to defending the truth of God's Word, many arguments should simply be avoided. It really doesn't matter who starts them, or often even who is right, the head of the house should take the lead in bringing them to an abrupt end. Many times, the way we handle an argument directly impacts its results. There have been times when I have pushed my point and no matter how hard I have pushed, there has been push back and I've failed to make my case. In other instances, I have quietly capitulated after making my point, only to have my opponent quickly see the error of their ways and come to my way of thinking.

Of course when dealing with young children, parents are generally always right to contend. The amount to which one contends in such situations will depend on the age of the child and the situation – the younger the child, the more the parent must assert their authority. While older children must respect their parents, as they learn to reason, we must accept that as they grow to maturity as adults, they will begin to have their own convictions. Hopefully, if your training of them was good when they were younger, the instances of opposing convictions will be few.

When we do need to end an argument, though it can often be difficult, the following verse must be our guide.

> And the servant of the Lord must not strive; but be gentle unto all men, apt to teach, patient, In meekness instructing those that oppose themselves; if God peradventure will give them repentance to the acknowledging of the truth; And that they may recover themselves out of the snare of the devil, who are taken captive by him at his will. (2 Tim. 2:24-26.)

Ultimately, it takes wisdom and experience to handle strife in the home and we'll never always make the right decision in this sinful body. We must simply continue in prayer and keep the above principles in mind. It is no wonder that the apostle Paul makes the qualification of elders in the assembly contingent upon a man's ability to rule his own house well (1 Tim. 3:5). This does not mean that an elder can't be childless, but it does mean that if he has children, they must be in subjection. Raising a family using biblical principles certainly gives one plenty of practise dealing with conflict and this can be very useful in the body of Christ.

Chapter 16

How Many Times?

With strife comes hurt and with hurt comes the need for forgiveness. Thus, I'd like to discuss this vital topic in this chapter. The apostle Peter came to the Lord to ask about this very issue.

> Then came Peter to him, and said, Lord, how oft shall my brother sin against me, and I forgive him? till seven times? Jesus saith unto him, I say not unto thee, Until seven times: but, Until seventy times seven. Therefore is the kingdom of heaven likened unto a certain king, which would take account of his servants. And when he had begun to reckon, one was brought unto him, which owed him ten thousand talents. But forasmuch as he had not to pay, his lord commanded him to be sold, and his wife, and children, and all that he had, and payment to be made. The servant therefore fell down, and worshipped him, saying, Lord, have patience with me, and I will pay thee all. Then the lord of that servant was moved with compassion, and loosed him, and forgave him the debt. But the same servant went out, and found one of his fellowservants, which owed him an hundred pence: and he laid hands on him, and took him by the

throat, saying, Pay me that thou owest. And his fellowservant fell down at his feet, and besought him, saying, Have patience with me, and I will pay thee all. And he would not: but went and cast him into prison, till he should pay the debt. So when his fellowservants saw what was done, they were very sorry, and came and told unto their lord all that was done. Then his lord, after that he had called him, said unto him, O thou wicked servant, I forgave thee all that debt, because thou desiredst me: Shdest not thou also have had compassion on thy fellowservant, even as I had pity on thee? And his lord was wroth, and delivered him to the tormentors, till he should pay all that was due unto him. So likewise shall my heavenly Father do also unto you, if ye from your hearts forgive not every one his brother their trespasses. (Mat. 18:21-35.)

Too often, when we are hurt, we focus in upon the crime committed against us. All we can think about is the devastating pain we are currently enduring. Sometimes we are physically scarred, sometimes emotionally and sometimes only our pride is really injured. The Lord Jesus gently but very firmly answers the apostle Peter in a way which should demonstrate to every Christian that we really have no option but to forgive, that is, if we really understand the extent to which God has forgiven us.

The New Testament talent was the largest weight used for currency. It weighed about 35 kilograms. One talent was about six thousand denarii. The average man's wage was about one denarii a day. Thus, a talent was about sixteen years' wages. Thus, the first servant's debt was about ten thousand times sixteen years wages, about one hundred and sixty thousand years' wages. Compare this to the debt owed by the second servant, one hundred denarii, about one hundred day's wages. The Lord Jesus was in effect saying to Peter, if you can't forgive the crimes committed against you, when your Heavenly Father has commuted your death sentence, you really haven't understood the gospel! Unfortunately, because we've minimized sin, and rarely preach about it in today's modern churches, that is the problem, we do not really understand salvation. If we did, we would willingly forgive and forgive, seventy times seven and continuously, since the crimes committed against us pale into insignificance compared to the crimes committed by us, from the time of our birth, against an impeccably holy God. We are instructed that we may rebuke our brother if needed, but we must forgive. The below verse sounds like we must wait for his repentance before we forgive, but as the Lord Jesus hung on the cross, He demonstrated that we must forgive, even when the other party is unrepentant (Luke 23:34). It is just that if the other party is repentant, the two-way relationship can be completely restored.

> Take heed to yourselves: If thy brother trespass against thee, rebuke him; and if he repent, forgive him. And if he trespass against thee seven times in a day, and seven times in a day turn again to thee, saying, I repent; thou shalt forgive him. (Luke 17:3-4.)

One of the reasons why we have ongoing strife in the church is because we do not follow the Biblical pattern given to us by our Lord to deal with such offences. The rule is, involve as few people as possible. First try resolving an issue one-on-one. If you are able to resolve the issue, no-one else need know anything! If you can't resolve an issue one-on-one, take only one or two extra people as witnesses to your attempt at resolution. Only if this fails do you take the issue to the church. We tend to tell as many people as possible, even before the person who has offended you may even know that they have done so.

> Moreover if thy brother shall trespass against thee, go and tell him his fault between thee and him alone: if he shall hear thee, thou hast gained thy brother. But if he will not hear thee, then take with thee one or two more, that in the mouth of two or three witnesses every word may be established. And if he shall neglect to hear them, tell it unto the church: but if he neglect to hear the church, let him be unto thee as an heathen man and a publican. (Mat. 18:15-18)

In the verse below, God's forgiveness of our daily, ongoing sin is dependent upon our forgiving our brother. I am not saying our salvation depends on this, but, in our sanctification, our fellowship with others and with God is temporarily broken until we forgive or make things right through confession of our sin (1 John 1:9, James 5:16). As I mentioned above, if we do not forgive, we haven't understood the extent to which we have offended God and the enormity of His mercy in forgiving us.

> And when ye stand praying, forgive, if ye have ought against any: that your Father also which is in heaven may forgive you your trespasses. But if

ye do not forgive, neither will your Father which is in heaven forgive your trespasses. (Mark 11:25-26.)

The apostle Paul also confirms this thought, and links bitterness with unforgiveness.

> Let all bitterness, and wrath, and anger, and clamour, and evil speaking, be put away from you, with all malice: And be ye kind one to another, tenderhearted, forgiving one another, even as God for Christ's sake hath forgiven you. (Eph. 4:31-32.)

The writer of Hebrews also addresses the issue of bitterness needing to be uprooted as it is often the source of unforgiveness. He warns us to be diligent. He also warns us that holiness is the opposite to such bitterness. He reminds us that if bitterness is not uprooted, many may be defiled, that is, relationships may be ruined and some people may be discouraged to the point of falling away.

> Follow peace with all men, and holiness, without which no man shall see the Lord: Looking diligently lest any man fail of the grace of God; lest any root of bitterness springing up trouble you, and thereby many be defiled; (Heb. 4:14-15.)

Chapter 17

Gratitude

While growing up, I thought that manners were simply optional customs which were taught by adults to children because of social convention, because it was the culturally accepted way to talk. As I reflect on this now, I realize that in particular, being thankful, is linked to humility. If we are grateful, we think in terms of not what is owed to us but what has been done for us as an act of mercy. Note well in the following account, ten lepers called the Lord Jesus "Master" yet only one, a stranger, returns to give the Lord thanks for what indeed was not owed to them, but what was conferred upon them because of the Lord's compassion and mercy. While we are not told, it seems reasonable that the other nine were children of Israel, which is why the Lord Jesus stressed that the one who returned was a stranger. In other words, familiarity breeds contempt and this must be dealt with. Gratitude is not a mere nicety for outside, which we may overlook in the home.

> And as he entered into a certain village, there met him ten men that were lepers, which stood afar

off: And they lifted up their voices, and said, Jesus, Master, have mercy on us. And when he saw them, he said unto them, Go shew yourselves unto the priests. And it came to pass, that, as they went, they were cleansed. And one of them, when he saw that he was healed, turned back, and with a loud voice glorified God, And fell down on his face at his feet, giving him thanks: and he was a Samaritan. And Jesus answering said, Were there not ten cleansed? but where are the nine? There are not found that returned to give glory to God, save this stranger. And he said unto him, Arise, go thy way: thy faith hath made thee whole. (Luke 17:12-19.)

In order to develop richer relationships, we need to nurture that humble attitude which recognizes that no-one owes us anything, especially God. This is why the Apostle Paul reminds us to "give thanks" in everything.

In everything give thanks: for this is the will of God in Christ Jesus concerning you. (1 Thes. 5:18.)

Enter into his gates with thanksgiving, and into his courts with praise: be thankful unto him, and bless his name. (Ps. 100:4.)

And let the peace of God rule in your hearts, to the which also ye are called in one body; and be ye thankful. (Col. 3:15.)

The Psalms are rich with numerous injunctions to give thanks to the Lord. King David, who wrote many of the Psalms, though he was rich in this world's goods, constantly reminds us to give thanks. This was because King David had, from the time he was a shepherd, learned to be dependent upon God and thus to humbly receive of the Lord. While the author of Psalm 136 in particular is unknown, it is an excellent example of a Psalm which earnestly encourages us to give thanks.

In our affluent society, where we often have the attitude of Nebudchadnezzar, who thought he had gotten to his place of exaltation through his own doing (Dan. 4:30), we have become too self-reliant rather than God reliant, and this has only lead to more selfishness, and selfishness leads to weaker relationships. The apostle Paul also makes the connection between ingratitude and a darkened selfish heart.

> Because that, when they knew God, they glorified him not as God, neither were thankful; but became vain in their imaginations, and their foolish heart was darkened. (Rom. 1:21.)

We must thus learn to give thanks to God and to each other, in order to maintain a humble attitude, which will aid as an antidote to selfishness.

CHAPTER 18

As It Hath Pleased Him

Over the years, I've noticed a troubling issue which causes much disharmony and undercurrent in a church. This obviously has a negative effect upon relationships within the body. The issue is the lack of recognition for other peoples' gifts. For example, in several churches I've been in, those who were evangelists thought that only their ministry was important and did not recognize the conviction which God laid upon another's heart to work in a different area of ministry, such as in exercising a gift of teaching, or helps, or pastoral care, etc. When this occurs, the one group thinks that everyone in the church should be exercising the same gift as them, and if they are not, or seem to have a different focus, they are spurned. Another similar issue is the expectation that all members be involved in all activities at all times. For example, a family with young children may not choose to attend certain ministry evenings because of the need for appropriate training within the home, children needing adequate sleep, parents being exhausted, etc. Rather than the rest of the congregation just concluding that the family is unspiritual, we should either offer some help, or accept the fact that there are differing seasons of one's life, and that at another season, they may well be very interested. Note the following verse, how a good shepherd gently leads those with young.

> He shall feed his flock like a shepherd: he shall gather the lambs with his arm, and carry them in his bosom, and shall gently lead those that are with young. (Isa. 40:11.)

We would do well to take heed to the apostle Paul's teaching on this matter.

> For the body is not one member, but many. If the foot shall say, Because I am not the hand, I am not of the body; is it therefore not of the body? And if the ear shall say, Because I am not the eye, I am not of the body; is it therefore not of the body? If the whole body were an eye, where were the hearing? If the whole were hearing, where were the smelling? But now hath God set the members every one of them in the body, as it hath pleased him. And if they were all one member, where were the body? But now are they many members, yet but one body. And the eye cannot say unto the hand, I have no need of thee: nor again the head to the feet, I have no need of you. Nay, much more those members of the body, which seem to be more feeble, are necessary: And those members of the body, which we think to be less honourable, upon these we bestow more abundant honour; and our uncomely parts have more abundant comeliness. For our comely parts have no need: but God hath tempered the body together, having given more abundant honour to that part which lacked. That

there should be no schism in the body; but that the members should have the same care one for another. And whether one member suffer, all the members suffer with it; or one member be honoured, all the members rejoice with it.

There are many gifts within a healthy body of believers and God has set the members in a given church. It is thus incumbent upon us to recognize the importance of, and encourage the exercise of, the diversity of gifts within the body and not expect everyone to be engaged in, or have the same conviction for, the same area of ministry. The important thing is that all members wholeheartedly exercise the gift God has given them, within the context of God's ordained gender roles, and according to the appropriate season of one's life. The following interchange between the apostle Peter and the Lord Jesus about the apostle John is very instructive, as is the exhortation from the writer of Hebrews. Ultimately, we should all be focused on the Lord Jesus and on following Him, not others.

> Then Peter, turning about, seeth the disciple whom Jesus loved following; which also leaned on his breast at supper, and said, Lord, which is he that betrayeth thee? Peter seeing him saith to Jesus, Lord, and what shall this man do? Jesus saith unto him, If I will that he tarry till I come, what is that to thee? follow thou me. (John 21:20-22.)

> Wherefore seeing we also are compassed about with so great a cloud of witnesses, let us lay aside every weight, and the sin which doth so easily beset us, and let us run with patience the race that is

set before us, Looking unto Jesus the author and finisher of our faith; who for the joy that was set before him endured the cross, despising the shame, and is set down at the right hand of the throne of God. (Heb. 12:1-2.)

CHAPTER 19

Who Has Your Heart?

This chapter is entitled "Who has your heart?" This is a crucial subject because who has our heart has our affections, loyalty, obedience and will and is the one with the greatest influence on our life. In discussing Biblical relationships, both in the family and in the church, it is crucial that we discuss this issue as it is often the source of why such Biblical relationships are in tatters.

The heart of man with its deep affections and motives can be given or stolen. Individually our hearts should be toward God. A son's and daughter's heart should also be toward their father and mother. A wife's heart toward her husband, a husband's heart toward his wife. When we covenant, our collective heart should be toward each other and collectively toward the eldership of the assembly, demonstrating loyalty and unity at all times.

> The heart is deceitful above all things, and desperately wicked: who can know it? I the LORD search the heart, I try the reins, even to give every man

according to his ways, and according to the fruit of his doings. (Jer. 17:9.-10)

The prophet Jeremiah teaches us that our hearts are deceitful above all things: We can both deceive others and be deceived. One form of this deception is often in relation to our loyalty, being deceived into misguided loyalty or trying to steal the loyalty of someone else from whom it should be directed. Though we may be aware of this truth, Jeremiah emphasizes this because we often are dishonest or ignorant of just how "desperately wicked" our hearts really are. Jeremiah asks, "Who can know it?" man may be deceived, but God is not. God searches the heart and tries the reins, like a horse rider attempting to gently guide a beast with its own will. He reminds us that God gives us according to our ways and fruit of our doings, not words or intentions.

When our heart is not given to the appropriate person, devastating things happen. Solomon pleaded for his son's heart (Prov. 23:26). We don't know which son he was speaking to but perhaps it was Rehoboam who later forsook the old men who stood before Solomon his father and instead listened to his peers. We don't know this but we do know that Solomon's son's heart was not with his father, prompting this plea.

> My son, give me thine heart, and let thine eyes observe my ways. (Prov. 23:26.)

These are words of desperation. If you read the context, Solomon was in effect saying, "Son, I've made many mistakes with women. Observe the consequences I have suffered. My son, give me your heart. My son, trust me, I speak from experience, don't make the same mistakes as I have."

> My son, keep thy father's commandment, and forsake not the law of thy mother: Bind them continually upon thine heart, and tie them about thy neck. When thou goest, it shall lead thee; when thou sleepest, it shall keep thee; and when thou awakest, it shall talk with thee. For the commandment is a lamp; and the law is light; and reproofs of instruction are the way of life: To keep thee from the evil woman, from the flattery of the tongue of a strange woman. (Prov. 6:20-24.)

We are exhorted to bind the commandment of our father and the law of our mother upon our heart. This word for bind is the same word used to describe the foolishness which is otherwise bound in a child's heart. So, through parents' training and discipline, we are to unbind the foolishness and bind on wisdom. Why is this? It is for this very purpose, to keep us from being wrongfully influenced by flattery or, too easily have our heart stolen.

Let us look at the flattering lips of a man (as it is not just women who can steal one's heart).

> And it came to pass after this, that Absalom prepared him chariots and horses, and fifty men to run before him. And Absalom rose up early, and stood beside the way of the gate: and it was so, that

when any man that had a controversy came to the king for judgment, then Absalom called unto him, and said, Of what city art thou? And he said, Thy servant is of one of the tribes of Israel. And Absalom said unto him, See, thy matters are good and right; but there is no man deputed of the king to hear thee. Absalom said moreover, Oh that I were made judge in the land, that every man which hath any suit or cause might come unto me, and I would do him justice! And it was so, that when any man came nigh to him to do him obeisance, he put forth his hand, and took him, and kissed him. And on this manner did Absalom to all Israel that came to the king for judgment: so Absalom stole the hearts of the men of Israel. (2 Sam. 15:1-6.)

Absalom stole the hearts, that is, affections, loyalty, obedience and worship that was due his father and directed it toward himself. He did not really have the good of the people in mind, but his own agenda. It is so wrong for us to steal the hearts of others and redirect their loyalty, obedience, love, and even worship, toward ourselves, intentionally or unintentionally. A son's (and daughter's) heart should always be directed toward his or her parents and toward God. When we care for someone's children' we must be careful not to steal the affections of them and draw them away from their God given authority. Young men must be careful not to steal the hearts of young women until those hearts have been given them by their fathers. Young ladies, Proverbs particularly warns against flattering lips. We must always redirect and focus each other's hearts back to their appropriate authority. There is only one antidote given in scripture to this and that is to obey the proverbs above.

David was partially to blame for losing Absalom's heart in that he did not deal with the sin of Amnon when he defiled Absalom's sister Tamar (2 Sam. 13). Michal did not give her heart to David, in fact, she despised him in her heart which cost her barrenness for the rest of her life (1 Chr. 15:29; 2 Samuel 6:23).

We see the blessedness of a heart given to the right authority in Solomon's early days as he writes:

> The king's heart is in the hand of the LORD, as the rivers of water: he turneth it whithersoever he will. (Prov. 21:1.)

The king gave his heart to the Lord which is why he was so fruitful. We read about this in 1 Kings 3:6-10:

> And Solomon said, Thou hast shewed unto thy servant David my father great mercy, according as he walked before thee in truth, and in righteousness, and in uprightness of heart with thee; and thou hast kept for him this great kindness, that thou hast given him a son to sit on his throne, as it is this day. And now, O LORD my God, thou hast made thy servant king instead of David my father: and I am but a little child: I know not how to go out or come in. And thy servant is in the midst of thy people which thou hast chosen, a great people, that cannot be numbered nor counted for multitude. Give therefore thy servant an understanding heart to judge thy people, that I may discern between good and bad: for who is able to judge this thy so great a people? And the speech pleased the

Lord, that Solomon had asked this thing. (1 Kings 3:6-10.)

Solomon went astray in his latter days because he allowed his heart to be stolen by multiple idolatrous wives. (1 Kings 11:1-2.)

For the commandment is a lamp; and the law is light; and reproofs of instruction are the way of life: (Prov. 6:23.)

Reproofs of instruction are the way of life. Do we like reproof? It is so easy to have our hearts stolen by those who do not reprove or correct us, always speak well to us, give us what we want and make us feel special (Prov. 27:6.). This is exactly what Absalom did but it doesn't mean that Absalom deserved the hearts of the children of Israel when David was their king and the one who was accountable to God for their leadership. Michal owed her heart to her husband and king regardless of what she thought of his actions before the Lord. Solomon's heart was stolen by women who God had expressly told the children of Israel not to mingle with.

In many churches, youth pastors and other leaders may inadvertently steal the hearts of children or youth from their parents. If you work with youth, be sure to encourage loyalty to their parents or guardians. This is why the Bible speaks so much about discipleship, and the education of children by their own parents. Age-segregated activities are now accepted as the norm even though such subcultures are rooted in humanism and are a relatively new phenomenon. Biblical wisdom teaches us that foolishness is bound in the heart of a child, thus, when you put a large number of children (or immature youth) together with few capable and wise leaders, this only breeds more foolishness (Prov. 22:15; 1 Cor. 15:33). This certainly does not foster respect for authority but on the contrary, encourages peer dependence.

Another increasingly worrying trend in many modern churches is the free affection shown between men and women who are not married to each other. This is dangerous and can easily lead to someone's heart being stolen. Prior generations were far more reserved in their public expression of affection, even between husband and wife.

Why is it so crucial for our hearts to be given to the appropriate person? It is God's design that our affections and will be a powerful force. Can God teach us when our affections are with the world? Can a father reach his son when his son's heart is with his friends? Can parents pass on their godly convictions to the next generation if their children's hearts are with their peers? Can there be unity in a marriage when a wife's or husband's heart is elsewhere? It is by God's design that His will is accomplished when our heart is given to the appropriate person or submitted to the right God ordained authority. Remember, the Lord tries our reins. Parents too try the reins of their children, do they feel resistance or willing obedience?

> But what think ye? A certain man had two sons; and he came to the first, and said, Son, go work to day in my vineyard. He answered and said, I will

> not: but afterward he repented, and went. And he came to the second, and said likewise. And he answered and said, I go, sir: and went not. Whether of them twain did the will of his father? They say unto him, The first. Jesus saith unto them, Verily I say unto you, That the publicans and the harlots go into the kingdom of God before you. (Mat. 21:28-31.)

We see here that the first son's heart was really with his father, even though he at first refused, his heart smote him and he repented and went whereas the second son's heart was not with his father at all, and he only gave lip service to his father. The danger of a heart and mouth out of agreement is so well demonstrated by the children of Israel who marvelled at the Lord's great works and acknowledged his great wisdom but still had hard hearts, so hard that the Lord marvelled at their unbelief.

> And he went out from thence, and came into his own country; and his disciples follow him. And when the sabbath day was come, he began to teach in the synagogue: and many hearing him were astonished, saying, From whence hath this man these things? and what wisdom is this which is given unto him, that even such mighty works are wrought by his hands? Is not this the carpenter, the son of Mary, the brother of James, and Joses, and of Juda, and Simon? and are not his sisters here with us? And they were offended at him. But Jesus said unto them, A prophet is not without honour, but in his own country, and among his own kin, and in his own house. And he could there do no mighty work, save that he laid his hands upon a few sick folk, and healed them. And he marvelled because of their unbelief. And he went round about the villages, teaching. (Mark 6:1-6.)

As alluded to in our opening verses, it is not only people who can steal our hearts but earthly treasure, whether it be physical or philosophical. (2 Tim. 4:3-4.)

> Where your treasure is, there will your heart be also. (Mat. 6:21)

Who has our heart? To whom have we given our heart? Have we stolen someone's heart from someone else to whom we should be directing it? As we saw earlier, Isaac demonstrated that his heart was with his father, trusting him fully as they went to offer a sacrifice with no lamb (See Gen. 22). Jephthah's daughter's heart was with her father when she agreed to remain single for the rest of her life because of her father's vow to the Lord (see Judg. 11:36.) The perfect example of a son who gave His heart fully to His father is of course the Lord Jesus:

> Then said I, Lo, I come: in the volume of the book it is written of me, I delight to do thy will, O my God: yea, thy law is within my heart. (Ps. 40:7-8.)

> My son, attend to my words; incline thine ear unto my sayings. Let them not depart from thine eyes; keep them in the midst of thine heart. For they are life unto those that find them, and health to all their flesh. Keep thy heart with all diligence; for out of it are the issues of life. Put away from thee a froward mouth, and perverse lips put far from thee. Let thine eyes look right on, and let thine eyelids look straight before thee. Ponder the path of thy feet, and let all thy ways be established.

Turn not to the right hand nor to the left: remove thy foot from evil. (Prov. 4:20-27.)

If this was not a critical subject, we would not be told to keep our heart with all diligence. Once our heart has been stolen, the ones who should be our greatest influence lose their ability to guide us. Once this occurs, we are ships lost at sea. Hearts wrongly focused lead to disunity, division and destruction in the family and the church.

When God tries our reins, will He find willingness? When we try our children's hearts, will we find willingness? When those reins are tugged, is it by the right influence? Can someone else grab the reins of our heart easily? Are we attempting to pull the reigns of another's heart? To whom have we given our hearts? For where your treasure is, there will your heart be also. Remember the story of Absalom. Let us be conscious of the influence we have on another's heart. Children, give your hearts fully to your parents. Husbands and wives, give your hearts fully to each other. As a church, give your heart fully to God and to the elders who are accountable to God for the feeding of our souls (Heb. 13:17; 1 Peter 5:2). Let us not allow gossip, slander, backbiting or discontentment to allow our hearts to wander or be persuaded from being guided by the rightful and God ordained authorities in our life. This is God's design and it is only when our heart is in the hand of the rightful owner that God can truly work to produce fruitfulness in family and assembly relationships.

CHAPTER 20

Conclusion

Relationships are one of God's most precious gifts to humanity. In order for us to most benefit from them, they must be nurtured in accordance with His design. Because of our sinful nature, we are inherently selfish. This means that while we all depend upon and desire good relationships, what we naturally do and say undermines them. This means that we must diligently and deliberately take steps to understand both God's design and our tendencies to work against that design.

As we have seen, the Bible gives us many examples of both good and bad relationships. It also demonstrates the long term consequences of wise and foolish decisions. Throughout its pages, from creation to consummation, God demonstrates the complementarity of the male and female through His design of specific gender roles. When we blur the distinction of gender roles and dress, our society quickly decays into androgyny and eventually homosexuality.

The family is the fundamental atom of society. It is in the family where gender roles are to be taught and lived out. The apostle Paul reminds us that good relationships in the church are dependent upon us learning how to relate correctly in the family. Indeed he reminds us that a father who has children in subjection is more qualified as an elder because of the experience it provides him.

As parents and church leaders, we must know God's design for the various relationships within the family, and deliberately and diligently cultivate an environment in which such relationships are encouraged and strengthened. We must be conscious of directing hearts to their rightful, God ordained authorities, and strongly discouraging activities where someone's loyalty could be misguided. We must encourage a culture of intergenerational discipleship, encouraging the older members to come along-side younger members in the family and church. We must be careful to encourage purity between brothers and sisters in the Lord, reminding them that they should see their relationships as siblings in the family. Brothers should cherish and protect sisters as much as they prize wisdom. Sisters should not slander their brothers. Older women should be respected as mothers and older men entreated as fathers.

We must be careful to promote an environment of worship in the home, being conscious that private sin breaks public fellowship. This includes keeping our word and teaching children to obey our word at our first request. We must learn to appropriately deal with strife: vehemently defending God's Word, but willing to capitulate or remain silent when a matter is eternally inconsequential. Our tongues are as dangerous as a spark near a fuel can and our hearts, being desperately wicked above all, need to be guarded with all diligence.

Finally we must understand the Biblical definition of love which we are commanded to have for one-another. It is not the love promoted by the media, nor even in many churches. God's love does not rejoice in wickedness but rejoices with the truth. Love corrects. Though our relationships will never be perfect this side of heaven, knowing what they should be is part of the battle and gives us a goal to diligently pursue. May we be those who make a conscious effort to honour God by nurturing godly relationships in the home, and in the household of faith.

www.ingramcontent.com/pod-product-compliance
Lightning Source LLC
Chambersburg PA
CBHW021130300426
44113CB00006B/370